THE SEEKER

On the Path to Spiritual Freedom

MODESTE HERLIC

Goiânia

Author's Editing

2023

I dedicate this book to my father for his love and wisdom.

"The seeker" is a dialogue about the heart's
wisdom, the present moment, and the way
back home.

Contents

The Kiss of the Absolute Father leaves no mark on the face of the prodigal son. However, the Soul is marked forever.

Kunda

The seeker of Life had wandered through the realm of men for many years. He was seeking a cure for the ills of the spirit. He had gone from continent to continent, walked through loneliness, lived with scarcity and abundance. He had done much, but all his efforts were in vain, for at his last destination, he was told that he had left the answer in his abode.

Thus, he returned to his homeland. There, a lonely traveler, sitting on the shore of the sea. Life had not been kind to him. He had traveled to many places in search of the answers of his heart. He knew within, something was wrong. "But how can the answer be in my abode? How can the Creator be in this place? Have I not seen everything yet? What could still be missing?" These were the questions that tirelessly resounded in his chest as he gazed about and saw only injustice, poverty, sadness, sickness of body and soul.

His city was in ruins, and although he knew that his answer was there, he could no longer stay. He had to leave again. He tried to convince his relatives to leave the Capital of the Central Lands, that land desolated by evil, but they would not.

The man turned his vision again to the vastness of the sea, thought a bit, and spoke to himself: "This time I am on the run. But am I fleeing from myself or men?" He could not answer the question, but it was clear to him that he was always running away.

He then continued his pilgrimage. And after leaving the Capital of the Central Lands, he headed for the mountains. At that moment, he did not analyze much; he did not think of routes. He started to walk, for he just wanted to get away from there. Time flew by, the seeker continued his journey when, at sunrise on the seventh day, exhausted, overcome by loneliness and hunger, an imposing mountain revealed itself to him. This sharpened the last breath of energy remaining, and he quickly gained the edge of Kunda, a village at the foot of the mountain. Eduardo remembered that he had once heard comments about a mysterious mountain near this village.

The men and women who inhabit Kunda, left the capital luxuries many decades ago for unknown reasons. They lived as peasants, devoting themselves to the land and the simplicity of life. No one knew much about them, for they were discreet.

Upon reaching the entrance to the village, the seeker lost consciousness. For it had been seven days of aimless walking. When he awakened, he found himself in simple, but comfortable lodging. Beside his bed, clothes and a note informing him to take a shower. The villagers were expecting him to join them for supper.

Eduardo, who no longer believed in kindness from men, found it all very strange. But he took a minute to thank the universe, then took a shower.

Already showered and in clean clothes, he left the lodge. People, very spontaneously, called him to sit at the table to share what they were eating. There was no ceremony or curious looks. No one asked him his name or what brought him there. They welcomed the stranger, free of charge, without any restrictions. He was a guest that nobody had invited.

After supper, his host, Mr. João, invited him to spend the night in the lodging where he had been earlier. Also, if he wished, they could talk the next day. Eduardo needed rest. After being welcomed and nurtured, he slept the best he had in years.

The next day, he woke up with a new countenance. It was a mixture of inspiration and curiosity. Later, he went to see Mr. João, who did not question him or make any assumptions. The man made it clear, that he would have to work the land just like everyone else, if he wanted to stay longer. The seeker understood his host's proposal, and the very same day, he went to the fields to work on the land with his host family. Cindi, Mr. João's youngest daughter, soon befriended the stranger. At every moment, she asked him questions about life and its obstacles.

It had been three days since Eduardo's arrival in Kunda, and he did not get close to the mountain that had welcomed him the first day. His hosts had told him the name and the legends of that mountain. It was called Samah, and it had an energy and magnetism that Eduardo did not yet comprehend. There was something mysterious about Samah. Whenever he passed by it, he observed its grandeur for a while. Then he continued his way to the countryside. On the fourth day, while contemplating it, he found himself amazed. "Nature is so majestic and, at the same time, so modest! It lives, hiding its perfection," he then thought. On the fifth day, something was about to change his life. On the way to the fields, he stopped as usual to admire the beauty of the mountain. There, amidst the birds singing, he suddenly heard a voice saying: "Long ago, the hills took on human forms to tell men of the exploits of their ancestors." With a surprised look, the seeker asked, "Who is it?" The voice revealed itself. It was a relatively tall man, dark eyes and short grayish hair. He dressed in a light blue robe, and his skin resembled the glow of chestnut. With a pleasant, golden smile, he seemed serene and willing to help anyone in need. "I am Haroldo, Samah's friend," replied the stranger.

"I've been around for a few days now, and I've never seen you. Are you part of the peasants too?"

"I am part of everything," replied the stranger.

"I am Eduardo, from the Central Lands."

"Nice to meet you, Eduardo. What brought you here?"

"Let's say that life brought me here."

"What is your plan?"

"I do not know yet. Only time will tell."

"If I were in your place, I wouldn't trust time."

With a carefree smile, Eduardo said, "I'm glad I am in my place."

"So foreigner, can you tell me if time runs?" the stranger continued.

"Yes, of course. Time does not stop. Like an arrow that aims at nothing, it moves forward. But what does this have to do with our conversation?"

"Then, son, only time will tell."

In a wry voice, Eduardo said, "That is my line!"

Always with a serene smile, Haroldo continued, "What about you? Do you also run?"

"Only when I am late."

"If you spent your whole life running behind time, how would your existence be?"

"It would be late, and I would be lost."

"Separate your thoughts from the notion of time. That way, you will not miss the right path toward real life. If you run after what cannot be possessed, it will escape you like the deer that flees from the panther. Protect your mind from illusion. In this way, you will become master of time, master of yourself and the world."

"I must say that it has been a great pleasure to meet you."

"The gratitude is all mine."

"I am running now, but I will be back to talk with you. It seems to me that your spirit is as great as your friend Samah. Where can I find you again?"

"Everywhere on the mountain. I will appear to you at the right time. Take care!"

Eduardo went to the field to work the land with a sense of well-being. Haroldo exudes wisdom, and this made the seeker excited. A short time later, he spotted a family united in song and joy through the murmur of the wind. The members of this family worked the land with courage and happiness. Eduardo did not understand how a family could be full and thrilled, living in a village with no buildings, vehicles, and professional growth. But they seemed entirely happy, without malice, and in this, there was nothing false. It was then that the seeker could not bear his curiosity and went to one of them to question, "Please! How can you be happy in such simplicity?" To his fascination, the other man replied, "Only Samah's friend will be able to tell you."

Even though Samah's friend told him that he would return at the right time, late in the afternoon, Eduardo sought after Haroldo. However, he did not journey far, because the wanted man suddenly appeared to him.

"Good evening, Samah's friend. I was on my way to meet you. I am a seeker who has doubts, inquiries, and many uncertainties. I noticed you speak with depth, and your serenity transmitted confidence to me. I felt that I could open up to you. Can we talk about some subjects that cry out in my soul?"

"Yes, of course!"

"I do not know the worlds of the Creator. However, I can see Its Manifestation within the universe. I traveled through the materiality of the world and met many men. But I was shocked to find out that most of them were unhappy, dissatisfied, and always wishing for one thing or another. They had everything, yet they still complained about life. For example, I will tell you about a man I knew named Roberto. One day I sat down with him to listen to him. He had a house but wanted a bigger one, he had a car but wanted a better one. He said that he got married too early and did not have the chance to explore the world. At the time, he had four children and loved them deeply, yet he said that having fewer children could help him save money. He said that being an engineer allowed him to have a good life, but he wanted to be a historian. 'History is the guardian of civilizations' spoke the man. He said he was happy with his life, but he never stopped complaining about it. These days, I am getting to know the people here. When I look right into their eyes, I don't see any hypocrisy. Their happiness seems sincere to me. Moreover, I am here, in front of a stranger, in a new place, unexpectedly opening myself. And my heart is saying that you are the only one who knows my answers. O Samah's friend, there are so many questions in my heart!" said Eduardo.

"Ask your questions, and I will answer them."

"Everywhere on the planet, the foreigner is either loved or hated. But, here in Kunda, the peasants received me differently. Unlike the rest of the world, I am not an outsider in Kunda, but a human being. For the first time, in an unknown land, I feel no different. I have lived my life in indifference. For many years, I learned to desire things and to frustrate myself for not getting them. I walked endlessly through various parts of the world, and when I found myself with no air to breathe, I drew from my afflicted heart the strength to continue. Amid all this sadness, my days offered me no relief. However, I have come to see men resting on the road of life. Many times, I asked myself, 'Why me? Why can't I have an easy life?' When I was a kid, my best friend Paulo used to say, 'You know, Eduardo, happiness is not for all men.' I always thought he said this because he had seen his home country sink into a civil war. But today, I was surprised to see that there are men happy with so little in life. My curiosity could not quiet, and so I came to a peasant and asked him: 'Tell me, what is it like to be happy in simplicity?' He said, only Samah's friend will know the answer."

"It seems that you are in search of happiness. You have walked all over the world, and today you are here, in the heart of the earth, still without an answer."

"I went after the cure for the troubled spirit. As time went by, I stopped searching for that, and began to take an interest in the Supreme Creator. However, the path I walked was full of discontent until I reached Kunda, where, despite the short time of observation, it seems that all beings are happy. Deep in my heart, I remain searching for the Creator. But at this very moment, the desire to know happiness is pressing. How can man be truly happy? How can he devote his whole life to the pursuit of happiness while walking around unhappy? How can the peasants of Kunda be content with so little, while men elsewhere yearn for well-being even though they live in opulence?"

Haroldo interrupted Eduardo, saying, "Surely, because these unhappy men imagine happiness as the purpose of life."

Eduardo inquired in a rush, "But isn't the purpose of life happiness?"

"If you think so, you are not wrong, but you are not right either."

Confused, Eduardo said, "If I am neither wrong nor right, where am I?"

"Tell me something: what makes a man a philosopher?"

"Obviously, the action of philosophizing."

"Are you saying that you have to philosophize to be a philosopher?"

"Yes."

"Just as one needs to philosophize to become a philosopher, one also needs to practice happiness to become happy. Thinking like this, how can I become a happy person if everything I see is the negativity of life?"

"I do not think so."

"As long as a man spends days and nights complaining about life, he will not know a happy existence. What matters is the journey, which is all the moments in life. Happiness is not the purpose of Life. It is the journey itself. When you are walking home, focus on the gently moving breeze. Turn your eyes to the sky and contemplate the grandeur of the Creator. Notice when the rays of the sun blend with the gray clouds. Walk around the mountain, communicate with the flowers. Observe the pilgrimage of the ants; the flight of the birds; the silence of the trees; the dawn and the fullness of the moonlight. There are so many beautiful things to experience. Without judging anything, live the present moment and you will find, in a simple whisper of the firmament, the happiness you have been longing for. And if you cannot touch it, see it with the eyes of your heart, and just like the light of a thousand suns, the ultimate truth will be revealed to you in the darkness of the night."

In a split second, the seeker remembered the words of old Bokô[1], carefully stored deep in his heart. As he stared in astonishment at Samah's friend, he asked, "Would you like to be my master? I will be your disciple, serve you willingly, and love your wisdom."

With a humble smile, Haroldo asked, "Who says that I am worthy of a master?" With great confidence, Eduardo answered, "I don't know how to explain it now, but it was the mountain. Samah told me." The master then replied, "So be it! See you soon."

Then the two men said goodbye. On the way back home, Eduardo tried to see in nature the marks of happiness. However, his mind would not cease longing for another dialogue with his new master.

---

[1] Old Bokô will be further explained.

At your core hides what is highest in all existence. So as you become master of yourself, you become master of the world.

The Traveler

One evening, Haroldo sat on the riverbank to observe life around him as he usually did. The river was called Sita, and it flowed to the delight of the inhabitants of Kunda. It flowed merrily through every corner of the village, thus allowing its waters to soften those lands. In this way, there was never a lack of fruits, seeds, and vegetables in the surroundings of Samah.

Although he was always aware of the present moment, Haroldo decided to remember his past that night. Perhaps it was because his inner search was very similar to that of Eduardo, the young seeker he had just met.

His new disciple's burning desire to sip a bit of the Absolute Truth, reminded him of himself. That must be why he expressed so much compassion toward the stranger. Or possibly, because a genuine master loves everyone, and judges no one.

In any case, Haroldo knew the importance of compassion on the road to self-knowledge. For him, love for one's neighbor is the ability to mirror oneself in another; the capacity to be one with the beings that cross our paths, the wisdom to embody the spirit of the universe, and the facility to carry love in your heart no matter what.

"The only way to know yourself is to know the world around you," murmured the man, looking at Sita, which danced in the sweetness of the night. Even though his voice was very soft, it echoed deeply through the wind that filled the space.

Many things happened in Haroldo's past, but at that moment, he only wanted to remember how he had met Reba, his master. Reba was the manifestation of a great soul, a majestic being.

It was a difficult time for Haroldo when misfortune gave him no rest. He lamented for not having the life he had envisioned. As he spent his days in the anguish of the spirit, his existence had become a heavy burden that he dragged under the sun. Nothing gave him peace of heart, a peace that he once projected as love toward people and the possession of things. The more he contemplated his fate, the more he realized that happiness did not lie in things or people.

He wondered where to find happiness, so precious to all living people. What bothered him was, above all, that such an abstract thing existed somewhere in the concrete world.

Long before, he felt abandoned by the beauty of existence, he stood before Samah and, with all his might, spoke the multiple names of the Supreme, seeking help. He shouted, making the breeze shiver. He wanted peace of mind and quiet in his thoughts. He attempted to comprehend the meaning of life. He wanted to know why loneliness and boredom burdened him so much.

However, life has given him no remission; he complained excessively, cried too much and mourned. Despite everything, his suffering remained the same.

Many days had passed in anguish, until he decided to change. One day, a mysterious man appeared in front of his house. He knocked three times. Haroldo quickly ran to the door, due to the visitor's insistence. The frustration on Haroldo's face spoke louder than the smile that invited the stranger to come in. Although the man noticed Haroldo's dislike, he smiled and was quite friendly.

"How strange! How mysterious!" thought Haroldo, as he kept his face closed to any kindness.

The visitor was a man of medium size, dark, drawn eyes, short black hair, with a goatee that made him look pleasant. He dressed in a dark red robe, and his skin color was reminiscent of the setting sun. He looked like the men from the Second Country of the Eastern Lands, whom people called travelers.

"What is a traveler from the East doing here in my house?" Haroldo asked himself.

Immediately after thinking this, panic immobilized him. For no apparent reason, he found himself stunned by his visitor. He thought again, "What do I do now? I let him in without asking. Now what?"

The stranger continued to smile, looking at him lovingly. There was something very different about him, something intriguing and beautiful. The mysterious visitor had no shadow. Haroldo observed him until he realized that his body emanated a dazzling light. It was a majestic being. When Haroldo perceived this, he found himself surprised, for he suddenly began to smile ceaselessly. His frustration with life and his suffering on earth, had dissipated in the soft air around them. He felt a light touch on his skin. It was a pleasant breeze that kissed his face. The happiness that he had searched for so long along the roads of existence had arrived at his home. It was the smile of a traveler, accompanied by a delightful wind, a caress from the cosmos.

Eduardo became paralyzed by staring at the splendor that was emanating from that mysterious being. He could not speak or think. In that instant, what remained was his hearing and sight. He could only see the light and hear the voice that came from that shining being. Mysteriously, he heard the words spoken by the traveler as his own.

Bright as a thousand suns, the magnificent being spoke in a soft voice. It was a delicate voice, and yet its resonance shook all things in its presence. The man said, "Beloved brother, my name is Reba. We knew each other long before time existed, but you forgot me. When the time came for you to remember yourself, you remembered nothing, for you denied me. Your story did not tell you that most of it remained in my memory, for I, unlike you, have not changed. I have remained the same since you left our Father's house. But I must tell you. In the depths of your heart, you will find the way back home. There, our Father and I will wait to welcome you. All this because since the dawn of time, we were One. And united, we will remain after the end of time. In the hereafter, we heard you call the Almighty Father by all names. Many times, I have listened to your cries in the loneliness and darkness of the night. Your affliction here below has saddened me. But know that I cannot save you from yourself, for there is a place in the cosmos where it was engraved, from the very beginning of creation, that only the soul can free itself from illusions. However, the love in your heart overcomes all suffering. That is why I have come to bring you the holy words — stop longing for material things and look within yourself. That being so, the mystery of life will be revealed to you."

When Haroldo regained consciousness, the traveler had already left. This episode marked his soul. From that moment on, he stopped complaining about life and began to observe it. While contemplating the world, he found himself in front of a famous painting. Here, he realized that the painting's perfection was not in the illustration itself, but the small details and elements that only the keen eye can notice. Thus, he understood that the meaning of life was in the minutiae of existence. Everything that seemed imperfect to him began to manifest a certain charm. The creation in its totality seemed beautiful to him again, for he had become a happy soul, like a child who finds joy in everything he sees, touches, and feels.

The traveler's visit had changed Haroldo's life for the better. From that moment on, he decided to do the same for his fellow human beings. Wherever he went, he spoke of Love, influencing others to perceive happiness in the details of existence, in the tiniest points of the Now.

The flight

A few days had passed, and Eduardo continued to assimilate everything that occurred around him. It was a mild morning, unlike the previous night when he was disturbed with many thoughts and confusions. He did not miss the opportunity to witness nature and its exuberant components. From the bank of the Sita River, he could contemplate the magnificence of the Supreme Creator.

The seeker had been preparing to see the world as it appeared to be, but that morning's stunt revealed another facet of that world. However, the truth being, there was nothing new, besides nature and only nature. The landscape view had always been the same. What had perhaps changed were the eyes of the observer. In front of such beauty, Eduardo had to close his eyes for a moment. When he opened them again, he witnessed the flight of an eagle in the sky over Samah. This episode led him to think about the concept of freedom. "When I transcend, I want to be free as an eagle," he pondered. Then, he felt the fragrant breeze of creation on his face.

That morning, he rejoiced as he experienced the feeling of freedom. In his eyes, there was nothing but stillness, for he knew that soon, he would join the master who would teach him about genuine freedom.

Suddenly Haroldo's voice made itself heard: "Good morning, son." Seeing the master, Eduardo expressed, "They say that communication between master and disciple is inevitable." Haroldo replied emphatically, "In spirituality, yes, but not always in materiality."

"Master, a moment ago, I witnessed the flight of an eagle, and it made me contemplate the concept of freedom. Soon I had a fleeting sensation of being free, but I have my doubts about it," said Eduardo.

"Like slavery, freedom is both physical and mental. Man cannot place himself outside of society. He is born, grows, and dies within it. All around, there are standards to follow, which influence his personality. Man thinks he is unstoppable, while his mind moves from one current of thought to another, without ever being free," replied Haroldo.

The two men were reflective for a moment. The master continued, "What do you think of a bird trapped in a cage? Is it free or not?"

"It is not free."

"Careful with such certainty, but let's assume you are right. Now, imagine that we opened the cage and asked the bird to leave. Two things could happen — the bird might want to stay with the owner for unknown reasons, or it might fly away. Right?"

"Sure"

"Now imagine that this bird has never seen another bird fly. So it ignores the purpose of its wings. Even though it is not in its cage, it would not know what to do or where to go because it has never had an example of what it could do. This bird is like the man who finds himself captivated by the standards of society. He is the one who identifies with his friends or neighbors and never with himself. He walks through the crowd without knowing where he is going or even why he is moving. He lives in comfort, content with the ideologies of others. He has not investigated the history of the ideologues but adopts their way of thinking. He believes he holds the truth. Yet, he ignores that the truth is always beyond what the eyes can see. The bird, just like such a man, is mentally chained, although it is free. Both need to fly," explained the master.

"But how could the bird fly? You said that it has never seen another bird flying. Just like the man, the bird does not know that flying is a possibility," replied Eduardo.

"Of course! The bird, in this condition, cannot see any other possibility than to wander inside its cage. Man, on the other hand, sees no other option but to be ordinary. He is comfortable in his mental prison and cannot imagine any different reality beyond. Now, imagine that the bird, in all its agony, wonders: Who am I? Why do I roam around? What is the purpose of my wings? What else can I do but wander?"

Haroldo paused for a moment while Eduardo remained utterly absorbed in his words. The master's phrases echoed in the air surrounding the river. They were sweet words coming from the majestic being of Kunda.

The master continued, "Self-questioning begins to raise the consciousness of the bird. By investigating itself, it discovers all the possibilities that life offers it. Man must do the same, he must stop being ordinary and learn to be himself, and then he will be able to explore the authentic worlds. Like the bird, he will be able to fly as high as possible and know the universe in all its magnitude."

"I understood that if a man becomes uncommon, he will know the authentic worlds, but won't this incompatibility between him and society cause him pain and suffering?" asked Eduardo.

"Yes, but in only one aspect."

"Which aspect?"

"If he decides to place himself outside or against society."

"How can man not place himself outside or against society when he decides to be different? I am confused."

"If you were in a society where corruption, although forbidden by the laws, became a conscious habit. Eduardo, with all your principles, would you commit acts of corruption in such a society?" asked the master.

"No, I would never commit an act of corruption."

"Doesn't the fact that you do not commit acts of corruption in a corrupt society make you exceptional concerning the rest of the people?"

"Yes, of course."

"Can I say that you are putting yourself outside or against society by not practicing corruption, like many other people?"

"Certainly not."

"Then, being uncommon within society, you may well live with more tranquility than uneasiness. And there are a few ways to do this. First, it is essential that you respect the laws that govern the order in society. It is not because I am exceptional that I should not respect the country's law. Only order maintains freedom, and no one can be coerced into being free. Secondly, you must always keep in mind that your freedom may clash with that of another. Therefore, your space ends where mine begins. I have the freedom to get drunk. However, I must do so consciously. In no way can I let alcohol drive me to the point of fighting, harassing women on the street, or causing accidents in traffic. Thus, I can control my freedom so that it does not encroach on others' boundaries."

Eduardo remained silent.

The master continued, "Back to the bird that has found its freedom and, by self-inquiry, has understood that it must explore the world. When in the air, it will understand that it cannot fly unconsciously, and the sky has its laws. It will notice that sometimes it cannot hover higher than its condition allows. It will realize that it cannot stay in the air forever and that from time to time, it must return to earth. It will comprehend that the rules on earth are not the same as in heaven and for survival, the reconciliation of the laws of heaven and earth must occur. In its cage, safety was not a concern, but outside, it understands that all freedom brings with it certain responsibilities."

"Master, just like the bird, does man also need to reconcile his laws with the divine laws?"

"Yes, necessarily."

"On the other hand, it seems that freedom without responsibility incurs libertarianism," said Eduardo.

"Exactly! There is still an important point that we must discuss. Do you remember the beginning of the story?"

"Yes, I do"

"So, imagine that the bird was never free. And that during its whole life, it has been in a cage. Is there a possibility that it is free being in pen?"

"I would say that it is not free, but I am no longer as sure as I was at the beginning of our conversation."

"Why?" asked the master.

"I know very little of birds, but of men, I can say a few things. I met a man in the Southlands who had spent more than eighteen years in prison for political reasons. I asked him what was his experience in jail, and he replied — at first, I had my doubts, but today I know I am free. It no longer matters where I am or what I do; my heart is always free."

"Did you understand what that man was saying?"

"It seemed to me that he no longer cared about the things of the materialistic world."

"Yes, it is true! For this man, nothing else mattered but the foundation of real life. And the most important thing was to know that everything, which materially worries, chains man. In the end, freedom is just a state of consciousness. In other words, we call it: Detachment. So if you want to be free, stop worrying about the worldly things. Love and observe everything. Do not judge, do not condemn. Look closely at everything that is inside and outside of you. By doing so, you will understand yourself and know the authentic worlds. You will be free. From what I said, remember one thing: only he who surrenders to life will live fully. That is abundance," explained the master.

The Secret of Sita

One day, while the seeker was on his way home, he felt the need to stop for a moment and contemplate the life around him. On the horizon, he could see golden clouds covering the peaks of distant mountains. The sun, as radiant as a child's smile, had set in the heart of the sky. The seeker's eyes traveled over all that was there, until they landed on the river Sita, that sacred stream, a gift from the Supreme Creator that permeated the land of Kunda. Stupefied, Eduardo stood there for a while, completely surrendered to the spectacle of Sita. The river had come from beyond the horizon — from far away to supply existence wherever it passed. Through observation, the seeker attempted to discover its secret.

The truth is that Sita flowed as it always had, serene and turbulent. Sometimes the dance of its waters resembled a breeze, though untouchable, caresses everyone's face. But sometimes, it exists as time which flows, travels to the unknown, interacting with millions of worlds and their civilizations.

A few minutes later, Eduardo smiled as he realized that the Sita river was very similar to life. He smiled again because he had discovered this only through contemplation, in the present moment and not by the thinking.

Through the stillness of the spirit, where there was no reverie, Eduardo had abandoned himself to life, and through simple observation, he understood one of the great mysteries of Creation. In this complete peaceful state, he pondered: "Is this the state of fullness of which the master spoke? The vibration in which one knows the answers without having to ask the questions?"

Since there was no one nearby to answer him, he continued his way home. Something within him changed. However, he still needed more experience to manifest this transformation in the physical world.

No need to cross the roads that cover the earth's face in search of the truth. Look inside yourself. There lies the charm of the universe.

The Heart's Path

With the sun blazing, the work in the field was challenging. That day Eduardo needed some time to rest — to rest not only the body, but also the mind. He then thought of Samah. The master once told him that only those who are on the top of the mountain will know eternal rest. The days that passed after this reflection were days of hard work for Eduardo, who tried to climb the mountain without success. One day, he took a moment off and tried again. Unfortunately, he failed. Somewhat discouraged, he stopped at the foot of the mountain, looked at the sky, and asked himself: "How can I find rest at the highest point of Samah if I cannot overcome myself?" With those words, he lay down on the ground while his mind kept churning. Thus, he remained for hours without finding rest.

Suddenly he heard a voice saying, "There is beauty around Samah that one cannot comprehend." The master went to the disciple, which is unusual in spiritual practices.

The seeker then, wondering whether to be annoyed or flattered, said, "I am surprised that you came to me because we both know that I have nothing to offer."

The master pretended not to hear the disciple's phrase and expressed: "It will rain today. And tomorrow, nature will recover its freshness."

"It's true" murmured Eduardo.

"Tell me, how was your rest?" asked the master.

"I could not concentrate on resting, knowing that there is great beauty waiting for me on top of the mountain. I could not stop thinking about who is behind it all. Just being at the foot of the hill, I find myself amazed at such greatness. Standing here, I look at the world and see infinity. They say that for everything, there is a cause, but looking at creation closely, I notice a certain emptiness. Nature is so green it seems that it has never aged. Yet, it has witnessed the history of the first men," said Eduardo.

The master remained silent.

Eduardo continued, "In my youth, I had this question: 'Who is behind all this?' I promised myself that I would find the answer and that is how I went wandering in the world. Today, I no longer feel the flame that inspired me, yet I feel the candle burning inside me. 'What is the why of it all?' I cannot tell. However, I feel something bigger in my core. I have been searching all over for a cure to the anxious spirit. I had many explanations but understood nothing. Some men said one thing, others contradicted them, and in the end, I retained nothing of value. Even today, the same question lingers in my heart: 'Who is behind all this? Master, we have not yet talked about the Supreme Creator, this Great Being, the Creator of creation itself.'"

"You do not need to look far, for even those who have gazed upon the beautiful face of the unmanifest do not know the words to describe the wonderful divine light. How can one speak of the things that exist without talking about the Supreme Being, the Creator of all existence?" said Haroldo.

"Master, your question makes me think of Love."

"Maybe it is because the Creator is Love. Don't you see?"

Eduardo nodded.

"As time goes on, you will realize that the Supreme is the union of all things, and that nothing exists without It," explained the master.

"What is the way to reach the Supreme?"

"It is the path that does not observe any division. In truth, every way reaches It, but only the heart's route will touch the heaven of the heavens."

"Every way leads to It. That was precisely old Bokô's answer when I passed through the Southlands. For the first time, I hear two men saying the same thing about the Supreme," said Eduardo.

"How interesting! Tell me a bit about this story," said the master.

"I would love to, but first, I would like to come back to the question of the Supreme Creator. In the First Country of the Eastland, I did not risk touching this subject. It could have cost me my life. Everywhere on the planet, men think that their multiple gods are real ones. They hate each other, fight with each other, and do not realize that they are saying the same things. The subject of the Supreme should always unite and never divide; should it not"

"In every civilization's history, there will always be Saints, as well as Messengers of the Creator. Only he who listens through the ears of the heart will recognize the various forms of one Creator," replied Haroldo.

"I understand."

"Eduardo, I heard that the people of the Second Country of the Eastland are moderate when they speak of the Divine. Did you notice this on your trip?"

"Yes, I did. I even had the pleasure of living there for more than eight years. But I was only concerned with the search for enlightenment. This search became an obsession for me. I think this somehow slowed my spiritual growth."

"Explain a little more."

"The masters, whom I followed at that time, said that enlightenment was beyond attachment. They said that I should know detachment before any step on the path to self-realization. The problem was that in eight years, I could never fully let go of desire.

It is more paradoxical than it sounds because my only desire was for enlightenment itself. I tried to let go of this desire, but I couldn't, and that's how I gave up the search for enlightenment. I remembered what we talked about that day when I watched the flight of the eagle. You told me, 'And the most important thing was to know that everything, which materially disquiets, chains man. In the end, freedom is just a state of consciousness. In other words, it is called: detachment'. Now I see that, during my trip, I was more imprisoned than if I were locked up at home. Because I could not let go of the fixed idea of enlightenment. I did not surrender," responded Eduardo.

Haroldo was silent for a moment and, after a sigh, said in a cheerful voice: "What about old Bokô? How was the story?"

The two men were sitting at the foot of Samah in front of a magnificent view of nature. Eduardo was about to tell the story of his meeting with old Bokô. However, he was in no hurry. There was, in his patience, a bit of the silence of the trees. As for Haroldo, no anxiety occupied his face. The master knew the impatient heart is not a good storyteller.

Old Bokô

Eduardo spoke about old Bokô, and the story is as follows:

It had been a month since I left the East for the South by ship. I hardly counted the hours to disembark. But the trip had not always been like this. In the beginning, everything seemed cheerful. In the early mornings, I would lean against the bow of the ship, looking out over the vastness of the sea. From time to time, I would quickly escape from the azure ocean to observe the clouds' refinement in the sky. This spectacle was one of the most beautiful, and every morning, I went to the bow of the ship to admire the beautiful scenery.

For more than a fortnight, I observed the infinity of the sea and thought beautiful words about nature. Everything was going well until one day, boredom defeated me. I stopped appreciating the beauty of nature, and all I wanted was to return to dry land. With this feeling in my chest, I locked myself in my cabin for the rest of the trip.

When I heard the call to disembark, I jumped up and soon found myself outside the ship, in the heart of the Capital of the Southlands. Without any difficulty, I got a room in a hotel downtown. Exhausted, I needed a good rest. After negotiating the hotel room, I jumped into bed in broad daylight, and fell asleep.

While I was resting, I listened to shouting people gathered under the hotel building in an abandoned lot. The euphoria was so great, that it deafened me for a moment. I got up with some frustration, hurriedly put on a T-shirt, and went to the window to see what was going on.

The people were grouped, forming a relatively large circle. Inside there were other men, or at least that is what I thought at the time. They were dressed from head to toe in multicolored robes. I realized, there was no way these beings could survive with their bodies so covered under a forty-degree sun. No man would be capable of such a feat. So, moved by curiosity, I hurried down the stairs and joined the people in the circle to see the spectacle.

These beings with human posture practiced the art of magic. They made things appear and disappear. They appeared in two or three places at once. The small ones could carry two vehicles while still walking smoothly. They were supernatural beings that demystified the art of magic for human eyes.

These beings transformed themselves into different animals and trees and soon returned to their seemingly human aspects. Besides being charming, they practiced magic with a certain elegance. The harmony of their movements formed a rhythmic dance. Their spin was according to the cadence of the drums and celestial chants orchestrated exclusively by the initiated. It was all extraordinary. A spectacle so unusual that I came to wonder whether it was all a dream or reality. And, to my amazement, it was reality.

If I remember correctly, the day before that day, still on the ship, my irritated personality thought of 'dancing' as a sum of aimless movements. But that day, I saw 'dance' to be one of the varied facets of art that overflows the motion itself. So I approached a man in the group that formed the circle. From his dress, he appeared to be a professor. I greeted him and asked, "Sir, could you tell me what is happening here?"

"These beings make magic happen. They show us that it is possible to touch the sky while on earth. It is proof that everything is possible for man," the man responded. He explained that this ceremony was to celebrate man's communion with the mystery —

the union of the individual with the Unity when the manifest joins the unmanifest.

I then inquired, "What are these beings that move in the middle of the circle?" The man stared into my eyes and, with a warm smile, replied, "They are ghosts of those who have departed. In our culture, death is not the end. It is the beginning. We are here today to celebrate our eternal life, for yesterday we were, today we are, and tomorrow we will be. Yet we never cease to be. How can death put an end to that which is not even born? Tell me, stranger."

I nodded, not knowing what to say. The spectacle came to an end. After the crowd had dispersed, I sat down on the trunk of a tree, at the center of the ceremony. Then I thought, "Life is beautiful. How can I get angry about such small things?" At no time, did I imagine witnessing such richness manifested. On that day, I felt deep gratitude for the opportunity to share that moment with those beings.

Suddenly, as I was sitting and submerged in a sea of thoughts, I heard a beautiful and charming voice, saying, "O stranger, have you crossed the ocean to behold the beauty of my land?"

More startled than surprised, I stood up abruptly and turned to see my interlocutor. He was an older man, thin and tall. Despite the pale expression on his face, he had a bright appearance. The green of his eyes reminded me of the splendor of nature. There was something mysterious about the features of his face. I realized that this person was unique.

He looked at me and said, "Life is sacred. So you must see in the ceremony, the consecration of all the things you do. In other words, be conscious of the Now, and then you will understand the meaning of existence."

At that moment, a man passed before us, talking to himself and gesticulating. Looking at the scene, the older man asked me, "Can you tell me who this man is?" Naturally, I answered that he was a madman.

Soon after, I could see a certain disenchantment on the older man's face. He looked at me lovingly and spoke, "Only a mad man can recognize the madness of his fellow man. Tell me, stranger, are you demented?" Instantly, I replied that I was not. He continued, "But then why do you judge a person you do not know?" I explained that it was because the man appeared crazy.

The older man looked at me gently. While never losing sweetness of his smile, he expressed, "You said this because you obeyed your thought. However, your mind may not know the truth, for it is a product of society's prejudices and beliefs. Instead of looking at the stranger, you preferred to look at your mind. What a shame! The truth is that that man was praising the Supreme Creator in a language that many do not know. You did not pay attention to that man's words, and, with your false belief, you have launched an offense to a stranger. Instead of acting in this way, you could have said, 'I do not know the man, but I can investigate who he is'. To behave in this way is to function outside the curve. It is to be authentic, to be true to yourself."

The older man continued his explanation, "Pay attention to the social conditioning that hangs over your choices and your tastes. To understand the design of Life, one must apprehend the illusion of the mind. Quickly, our reasoning holds us captive, and we are not aware of it because we build the prison ourselves — our prison. We then hand over the key to the jail to our mind and pay it with the currency of our lust for fame, money, and power. So it can keep us in comfort in our mental cells. Ironically, the ignorant prisoner believes he is master of his mind."

"How can one discipline the mind?" I questioned the older man. He said, "If you do not control the mind, it will manipulate you, and one of the ploys it will use is 'fear'. It will make you think that you cannot be happy without satisfying your ephemeral pleasures. The game of Life is on, and you covet those things you should not until you become a slave to the flesh. These desires represent the chains by which the mind holds you captive. But it is not only you who go through this. I was once a slave to my mind."

The older man told me how he had been a slave to his mind and finally articulated, "I became master of myself when I began to love my neighbor, whether he was from the North or the South. At that moment, I realized the freedom that flowed in my heart. So I decided to go in search of the Supreme Creator. But in the middle of the road, I gave up and returned home."

Surprised, I inquired the reason for that decision. To which the older man replied, "Because three things changed my conception of Life — through the smile of a child, I noticed the love that links the Creator to creation. In the silence of the desert, I heard the heavenly voice. The one that had always guided me since that time when the universe was unmanifested. In the darkness of the night, I saw the light of a thousand suns. The brightness that never fails to illuminate the night of those who walk the path of the heart."

I further asked what the path of the heart is. The man answered that it is the route that leads the prodigal son to the Absolute Father. It is the path of Unity, the highway that knows every road. In truth, every pathway of Life leads to the Supreme Creator.

Naturally, I had to question him why our parents teach us to constantly choose between the duality of good and evil if the path is already One. To which he replied, "Observe the human paradox when man clamors for the exactness of his mathematics, while he cannot define the infinite that goes from 1 to 2."

At that moment, I felt the need to pose one more question, "Are you saying that reality is what we cannot see?" He agreed, saying, "Yes, the Ultimate Truth is that which is unmanifested."

"Without words spoken, I continued listening to the older man. With his green eyes turned to the sky, he asked me, "Why have you come here searching for that which the forms do not contain? Why not let the sweet melody of your heart guide you home? There, what you have forgotten awaits you."

Unresponsive, no words could flow out of me. I contemplated the older man's wisdom as I lent him my ears. He went on to say,

"One day, at the foot of a mountain somewhere in this world, not far from your heart, you will find the way to your truth. And you will soon recognize the messenger of the good word. However, remember not to get attached to the mountain nor the messenger. For only you can walk to your heart. This will happen when you understand the law that governs all laws — the Law of Love. Now go to your home."

In the older man's eyes, the truth rested. As I looked at him, I knew in that instant that I had to return to the Central Lands — to my home. Then I asked him, "O wise man, what is your name?" Nonchalantly, he said, "For you, I will be old Bokô." A few days later, I took the road back home.

Master, that is the story of my meeting with old Bokô. However, I do not comprehend much of what he said to this day. I think I understood the meaning of the sentences literally. Even so, I can still feel the marks of those words engraved in my heart. For now, I know that I lack the intelligence to perceive the Truth of truths.

The drops of sweet rain began to wet the ground. Haroldo looked at the disciple and said, "The rain has come. Observe it, and you will find in it why the wise men speak in riddles."

After saying these words, the master left. The disciple kept silent, trying to be one with heaven. Sitting at the foot of Samah, he attempted to unveil the secret of the rainfall. Soon he realized that the set of drops formed the rain, but each water particle was unique and complete.

When you love the son, you love the father too. So if you desire the love of the Supreme Creator, learn to love all Its creatures. All, without exception, from the stone at the mountain's foot to the bright star in the sky. Learn to love all things, animate or otherwise, for in them lies the pint of the Universal Artist.

The Division

One night, nostalgia overcame Eduardo. The memories of his family and loved ones took away his quietness. He remembered moments of affection, reciprocity, and celebration. This warmed his heart, but it also made him homesick. He missed that love. With this feeling vibrating in his chest, he looked for the master, and the first thing he said when he found him was, "Until today, we have talked about countless subjects, but I have not yet asked you, specifically, about love. Master, tell me about love."

"How can we talk about everything without talking about love since love is everything?"

"I am not talking about transcendent love. I am talking about the love that unites human beings, the love that creates civilizations and founds societies, the love that emanates from human relationships. We haven't said anything about that."

"We have the vile habit of fostering division where there is Unity. We don't realize that we are part of a system and that we form Unity itself. The false ego has deceived us, and since then, we have sought to distance ourselves from the Earth that gave us birth. Our desire to be individuals is voracious. We do not understand that being an individual means to be conscious of oneself in a structure. We are like the prodigal son who forgot his father's face. Why separate the transcendent from the immanent? Don't all things stem from the same source?"

"I can't understand it."

"Society has created standards of love, conventional ways of seeing love among human beings. First, you have the love that connects them to the sacred, and already there, they have fostered divisions. One says that the North's creator is the best, another says that the South's creator is even better. Each one tries, in some way, to impose his creator on others. Human madness didn't stop there. It has made man think that love for one's country is synonymous with superiority over neighboring lands. All around, we erect borders. All that the child of the motherland wants is to be superior to the neighboring country's children. If this is not enough, he wants to take possession of his neighbors and enslave them.

"Worse still, foolishness has overflowed our multiple personalities. In this state of consciousness, one no longer makes a point of taking one's hatred outside one's borders. One can now hate his brothers, the children of the same homeland. Then we create labels and privileges. Discrimination becomes normality, and the so-called fortunate one shows off. He says to his servant with a haughty bust: 'Look at me, I am your master, I am the best of men.

"Still under the yoke of the passions, men understand that love between two people must necessarily conform to society's conventional standard. Anyone who voluntarily or involuntarily places himself outside this standard will be excluded and rejected by society. Is that true love?"

"I think that true love should always unify people. It should not instigate hatred or division."

"So tell me: why did you start by separating love from its origin? Can any building stand without foundations?"

"No, but our perception of love is what we have been taught."

"I, too, have been in this position. People taught me to swallow everything and question nothing. This is how we live in society. However, there is no way to divide that which is indivisible. You cannot reach the light by walking through the darkness. Those who love, love, and there is nothing divisive in the act of love. In the perfect state of mind, all that man desires is to love and live in simplicity. The father then realizes that all the children of the nation are his. Similarly, the motherland son comprehends that the love and respect given to the neighboring motherland's son would bring peace to his kingdom."

"Some of my friends will say that this is utopia, and that man would never reach this state of tranquility."

"Men are proud. They no longer believe in the universe but trust in themselves. Whom would they be without the universe that contains them?"

"They do not realize that they are also parts of the universe. They disbelieve in everything and, therefore, in themselves. I perceive great confusion there. However, they will say that they are realistic and that we are dreamers."

"He who has lost everything does not realize that he has himself. He laments his misfortune, lives in the past, becomes a victim of the present, and hopes that the future, unknown to him, will offer him good fortune. The same thing happens to the person who believes he possesses everything. At no time does he realize that he does not apprehend himself. He says that he is knowledgeable and lives in the reality of things, but he ignores the truth that occupies his heart. He has not yet realized that his reality of things is an illusion, since he lacks the self-knowledge to complete what is already known."

"How can such men understand Love?"

"The path of procrastination leads to death. Therefore, instead of experiencing it in the present moment, he who desires Love will be directed to despair."

"How so?"

"It is simple. The being that puts his happiness in the hand of an uncertain future, will live in frustration because one never knows when the future will appear. One cannot believe that one day man will become genuinely lovely. What one must do is to experience Love, starting with each one of us right now, and right here. Those who have no kindness in their hearts call themselves realists, because they believe that man cannot love his neighbor. Because they identify with this common way of thinking, they think we cannot have a loving world one day. Because they are unaware of their reality within a larger structure, they ignore that change could bring a difference in the world, for to change within ourselves is to change the world that comprises us."

"I realize that man's materialistic view has made him blind. Exacerbated intellectualism makes him seek to know everything except himself. How ridiculous is he who, not knowing himself, boasts that he knows the Supreme Creator and His worlds? What imbecility!"

As if on cue, the two men laughed softly. Then, with serenity, the master said: "Eduardo, it does not matter how men organize themselves. Whether in a family, society, or civilization, love must not create division. So, as you said, love must always aggregate and unite. In the wisdom of a non-judgmental mind, Love only loves, does not question, and does not complain."

"Basically, we have to discipline the mind to reach a state of total tranquility as far as living in society is concerned."

"Exactly! And come to think of it, we already talked about this a few months ago."

"I remember, yes. But beyond that, I would like to know how couple love works. For example, how can two people come together to start a family?"

"We should not create standards regarding the organization of a family, a society, or a civilization. Love is free and always reflects Justice. Therefore, men can love in any way they please."

"By uniting love to its genuine source, I realize that it can only bring joy and peace and that there is nothing in this world that can corrupt a true love relationship. Nothing can stop genuine love, not even the circumstances of life. The nostalgia that ached in my heart, and the distance that eroded my stillness, have just turned to joy. I can say that I love my family and that this love is reciprocal. Even better, I feel the warmth of this green nature that currently surrounds me and reminds me that the world is beautiful. At this very moment, I understand that Love abides in all things if we allow ourselves to see with the eyes of the heart."

"I am happy to see that you have learned the lesson of Love well. Now tell me, how can two people experience love in a world of madness? How can they form a family in the heart of a corrupt and unfair society?"

"In trying to answer such a question, I observe nothing but fear. Fear should not encourage two people to start a family. When I speak of fear, I imagine the torment of loneliness, the weight of the standards and labels created by society, and the lust for power, fame, or money. In a community where corruption rules men, people must learn to unite out of Love and not fear."

With a brief silence as a sign of not knowing what else to say, the seeker looked attentively at the master and continued, "Following this conversation, I find myself able to talk about love. However, I know nothing about fear, except the suffering it causes me every day."

With a sudden yawn, the master expressed, "They say that the night is a good counselor. We should not waste its advice. Maybe it can teach you better about fear."

Ironically, Eduardo replied, "The night I know does not go through a thousand paths to claim its right. I imagine that the master is tired, and so is the disciple. Good night!"

"Take care!" the master returned to him.

The disciple then left the master's house toward his dwelling. His hurried steps in contact with the leaves of trees, fallen on the ground, intoned a melody softer than the silence of the night. But for unknown reasons, the stranger began to fear, and along with this fright, he walked home from the mountain. When he reached his room, he lay down to wait for sleep — a sleep that was slow to come, as anxiety awaited at the foot of the bed.

The world around you is a reflection of what is in your inner world. So, love and care for THE ALL. And THE ALL will love and care for you.

The Fear

That day, after waking, the seeker headed straight for the mountain Samah. The previous night had not been joyful for him. All he had wanted was a night full of advice. What he got was a legion of fearful thoughts. The master, as always, seemed to be waiting for his disciple at the foot of the mountain.

"Master, yesterday I expressed my doubt about fear. Since then, it has accompanied me every minute, preventing me from resting my mind and my body. I cannot stop thinking about it. This mentalization is automatic, and I want to get rid of it," said Eduardo.

"I can imagine how difficult it must be for you. Tell me what you think about fear," replied Haroldo.

"I think that fear brutalizes some men, while making others fearful. Whether a man is brutish or fearful, fear has made him a coward. We are so afraid that we do not want to risk being who we are. I want to share what occurred to me during my passage through Kala, the city of passions."

"Please tell me."

"From the very name of the town, I imagined that my passage there would be brief. Little did I know that there, in the City of Passions, I would meet the person who would enchant me the most during all my wanderings through the world. There I met Emma. A graceful woman with a deep, honey-colored gaze. Her walk was a dance for my eyes, her talk a melody for my soul. And when she smiled, she made me believe that the whole world was there, beside her, not to mention her heart, kind, generous and trustful in humanity. We experienced a beautiful romance. It was such a perfect love story that it almost made me forget everything that was going on in the city around us. The lust and the exacerbated needs of the people resulted in many discords, fights, barbs exchanged, and physical aggression. At every moment, there was some manifestation or complaint from someone who was not satisfied with what he had. Kala's people always needed more. And when they did not get what they wished for, they took out their frustrations on others. I lived in Kala for about a year. When I realized that it would be impossible to continue experiencing all that disorientation, I invited Emma to leave with me. To my dismay, she refused. Although she loved me, she said that Kala was also part of her. Furthermore, she still believed that everything could get better, so she would stay there with her family. I, then, continued on my way, leaving that love behind. You know, master, at the beginning of my youth, I thought I would have a more conventional life, I would graduate in Engineering, get married, have children, and live well. As time went by, this thought became distant from reality, and I have trodden my path only in solitude. I always missed someone to share and live life's discoveries with me. But after being so disillusioned with human affairs, I gave up on this aspiration too. But meeting this gentlewoman in Kala, I felt for a moment that the will to experience love resurfaced within me. So having to leave that city without the woman I still loved, hurt me too much. It was the pain of leaving her, the pain of being alone again, and the pain of once having felt love and letting it slip through my fingers, which are now cold and empty. These thoughts, this fear of loneliness, have visited me tonight, taking away my quiet. Master, do you think that this love might have been genuine, or was it attachment to desire? And about the fear of being alone, did I create the need to have a person with me?"

"Your time in Kala was very intense indeed. However, it was also a courageous decision to leave. A wise man once said, 'The greater the needs that a man creates for himself, the proportional is his degree of dissatisfaction with life.' You see, maybe you did not consciously forge this longing for love but reproduced what society has been teaching men for millennia. We are instructed to have desires. And, after meeting them, we cling to them, despise them, and go in search of new ones. Most people identify themselves only with material things. By loving the possession of things, man moves from the state of master to slave. In the reasoning of his greedy mind, he ends up making himself one with his possessions. In this emotional state of material and absolute dependence, a simple scratch on one of his possessions is considered an offense to his person. He then becomes capable of the worst atrocities. He offends, corrupts, lies, steals, robs, and kills with the sole purpose of possessing things. Now, observe the following situation — the husband thinks his wife is a thing to possess. One sad day, he feels insecure about their love story and murders his half."

"What a paradox! How can one love and hate at the same time? I cannot understand it."

"Pure Love is the point of convergence between divergent concepts that constantly aggregates and integrates the path to Unity. We see the manifestation of such Love in love relationships or family relationships. But these are still a worldly manifestation, therefore subjected to the law of duality. It turns out that the husband who comes to cause his wife suffering has never really loved her. In this kind of illusory love, there is less than a step between passion and hatred. Today we love, tomorrow we hate, and the cycle repeats itself until it becomes natural. Faced with this, we think, 'That's just the way love is. It's not perfect.' However, this belief is fallacious. In our present age, it is difficult to separate man from the material. Materialism has invaded all human concepts to such an extent that even before we relate to other people, we need to create a certain expectation of them. When they fail to meet our expectations, we become frustrated, and then what was once love turns into hate," answered the master.

"And what about Emma? Was it genuine love?"

"We usually think that other people should complete us. We ignore that we are already complete beings, and we certainly do not need to join with others to experience love. Love is not outside of us, but within. On the other hand, it is always good to bond with other people, whether by professional or loving relationship or friendship, because that is a way of becoming truly human. I believe that you should not worry so much about labeling the kind of love you have felt. The more you try to understand it rationally, the more the fear of loneliness can bring you down. Remember, we are whole beings, inserted in the Unity. Inside the Unity, there is no fear or loneliness. In the Unity, there is only Love. If you open yourself to that universal truth, everything that happens in your life will be right. If someone comes to be with you, it is right. If someone leaves, it is all right too. It is the movement that gives meaning to life. That dance cannot stop."

"I understand"

"Now, tell me, what do we do in the face of fear?"

"We dress up as personalities alien to our True Self. Everywhere we go, we act like actors or actresses so that society can accept us. Many characters are boiling inside us that we no longer have any idea about who we are. O master, how miserable is the man who fears to become himself, clinging to his image, people, things, professional and social status? Every moment of our lives, our mind reminds us that we can lose something. The mind never tires of tormenting us with so many fears. As time goes by, reasoning in this way becomes natural to man. Master, how can we annihilate attachment?"

"If you want to tame attachment, you must practice detachment."

"To get rid of the fear of losing my family members and the people I love, should I then move away from them?"

"No, not at all. Only in the balance of Being is the excellent practice of detachment. It is like a mother who loves her son intensely but must let him marry another woman to move on with his life. The fact that the mother allows her son to leave with another woman does not mean that she does not love him. This is precisely the example of true love because there is nothing selfish about it. Do you understand?"

"Yes, master."

They fell silent. Haroldo smiled with satisfaction. Eduardo stood up, and through his eyes, one could see the happiness of drinking from the fountain of wisdom that emanated from his master. Deep in his heart, he knew that this was a majestic being. He then thanked the great teacher and went to the field to work the land. After his toil, he returned to meet his master. As for his fear, there were still some doubts to be lightened.

Meditation and Contemplation

In the sky, neither bright nor dark, the sun was slowly saying goodbye to Kunda, while its golden rays painted the most beautiful picture of existence in the eyes of men. Samah itself became a mountain of gold and shone as if it were the only one in the world. The night was on its way, and the entire city seemed to await its sweet darkness since everything in it was immersed in profound repose.

Sitting at the foot of the mountain, Haroldo and Eduardo delighted in the magnificence of creation. It was all stunning, all lush and enchanting. After taking great delight in this divine food, meant for the eyes of the heart, the master said: "One can find the Supreme's splendid face in the union of night and day. Look up to the sky; there is the countenance of the Soul of the world."

The seeker observed the firmament, and soon, his face was illuminated, for he was witnessing the Supreme Being's grandeur. After a deep breath, followed by a sigh as soft as the dawn, he manifested: "I feel the presence of the Universal Soul. Although I do not know It, I can feel It."

The master watched the landscape in silence. After a moment, Eduardo came out of his reverie. He continuously smiled, as if all doubts had disappeared from his mind.

Luckily for him, the master was there. He knew that a short moment of happiness was not enough to put an end to fear. It was necessary to act before this disease of the soul. That 'acting' was nothing more than the dialectic that makes it possible to understand the world. Then Haroldo said to his disciple, "What doubt left in your mind about fear?"

Like a spring breeze, the beauty of the universe had come from far away to caress Eduardo's face and soften his heart. Thus, he was calmer and more willing to know how to overcome the reign of fear in his life. With this quietness of spirit, he answered the master, "First, I understood that we must see the leading cause of our fears. I am afraid of death because I do not want to lose the facilities that life affords me. Since fear does not stop bothering me, I must seek relief through detachment. How can I practice detachment? For that, should I abstain from the things of life?"

"First, remember that intemperance brings misery. That is precisely why we should seek balance in everything we do. If you practice detachment excessively, you will do nothing praiseworthy but sink into yourself."

"In that case, what can we say of the wise men who isolate themselves from the world and devote themselves to an exclusively sane life?" asked Eduardo.

"No one knows the reasons that lead the wise man to isolate himself from the world except himself. Now, if we want to better practice the Law of Detachment, we must, first, obey the Law of Love. Let us imagine that a thousand men find themselves in a gloomy place, all enclosed, where the only things experienced are affliction and darkness. In that place, men are angry with each other; they only live by wickedness. To those men, it was said that only he who best practiced the Law of Detachment would have the spiritual freedom to rise. One day, one of them went out of that darkness to discover a luminous and happy world outside. He saw the light of a thousand suns and experienced the divine glory outside the darkness. Would he be selfish if he decided to keep the light for himself?[2]"

"Yes, he would be selfish and, as far as I know, a selfish life is a life without glee," replied Eduardo.

---

[2]Inspired by Plato's Cave in Republic (514a–520a).

"The wise man who distances himself from the world practices the Law of Detachment perfectly. However, he misses, in a way, the opportunity to elevate consciousness across the globe. Caring for someone's spiritual health is the greatest gift that life can offer us. I am not saying that the wise man who lives far from society is selfish. But I know that a spiritual man among the masses can bring much wisdom to humanity, for the ignorant will have the opportunity to learn by example."

"So, master, how can one objectively practice detachment in all its balance?"

"Our restlessness begins in mind. One must learn to discipline it. Attachment creates fear, and soon fear is incorporated into the mind. Then comes the agony of fearing everything without ever being conscious of our stupidity. For example, when you find yourself alone on the street and fear that a thief will appear. Just as magnets attract themselves by the contradiction of their poles, if I constantly vibrate in fear, I will attract that which I fear the most. If I spend weeks or years of my life in fear of a specific disease, there is a great probability that it will finally install itself in my body as a matter of energetic affinity. That is why, the moment your mind begins to materialize a probable danger, what you should do is to exercise some control over it and tranquilize it. If you can totally take away the fear at that moment, then do so. In this way, you will calm your mind, and everything will become clearer little by little. You can also do exercises for the awakening of consciousness."

"Can you further describe the process of mind control?"

"As far as I know, mind control mechanisms pass by mental skills such as mindfulness, intelligence, and attention."

"Mindfulness requires us to put presence in what we do. By practicing it, we place ourselves outside of patterns and consequently become authentic. For example, I will not get married because society says it is the right thing to do. I will do it because it is the best thing for me. From the same perspective, Intelligence is the ability to choose the thought that would be the object of mental fluctuations. In other words, it would be the ability to discern right from wrong. For example, to always think positively and not let any hateful thoughts invade the state of mind. This is not easy at first, but it becomes natural to act in such a way over time. Finally, Attention helps us educate the mind. It is the sensor that is around mental activity. Its job is to observe the negative deviations of the mind and regulate them automatically. For example, if I am on the street and I see some stranger, usually the first thing that comes to mind is, 'I do not trust that man.' At that moment, Attention should help me order my mind. I can internally respond to it: 'Look here, chattering mind, you do not know him, so do not judge him. Now ask the Creator that this stranger be blessed.' As you do this, you will gradually take control of your mind. Somehow you will begin to observe your own thoughts and therefore the greed of your mind. From this day forward, you will no longer be the observed one, but the observer. You will be the cause of the events in your life and not its effect. At that point, it becomes difficult for the mind to feed fear, as it no longer controls the thoughts. In short, free yourself from the trick of the mind and you will become master of yourself."

"What kind of exercises for awakening consciousness can help in this process?"

"Meditation and Contemplation, for example."

"How do you do Meditation and Contemplation? What are the rules?"

"There are no specific rules for doing these exercises. It is effortless. To meditate, find a nice place to sit, away from noises. Then close your eyes and dedicate yourself to silencing your mind. Focus your attention on the point of equilibrium that connects the two eyes, just above them. Observe the mind and its fluctuations, not holding on to one thought or fighting another, just letting emptiness run through your infinite spaces. Little by little, the greedy mind will discipline itself and leave its atmosphere more tranquil and serene. Here comes a powerful consciousness filled with love and compassion. As for Contemplation, the procedure is almost the same. One might think that Contemplation is an even more complete exercise of spiritual elevation. Contemplation consists of paying attention to everything around you without losing your center. This is to be aware of the 'Now', the present moment. During the day, contemplate nature, the trees, the beauty of a flower, the smile of a child, the flight of birds, etc. When night comes, take a place before the darkness that frightens those who hate life and close your eyes. In that way, with the eyes of the heart, you will see the splendor of the Genuine Being. You will then know the supremacy of heaven and never again be bound by the chains of the earth."

As a sign of devotion and reverence, Haroldo stopped for a moment, looked at the sky, and said:

"O Great Soul
I know that Your Love
rules over Creation
which is also Yours

There are thousands of wonders
for the eyes of Love
Therefore, my heart is afflicted
in the kingdom of men,
for they prefer to covet"

After having spoken, the master continued his explanation, "Contemplation can be accompanied by chanting a mantra or just by the silence of the mind. You can do it with your eyes open or closed. The important thing is that you are at peace with yourself."

"Can you give me some examples of mantras?"

"OM, HU[3], or even GOD are great mantras. Pick any high vibration word that you like, and that makes sense to you."

"I can see."

"Finally, these mental mechanisms are ways of observing life around us without ceasing to be at the center of ourselves. My son, meditate all the time, even when you are walking on the street. And above all, don't miss the chance to contemplate the Unity in all things. There is always something of the divine plan going on."

"Master, Meditation and Contemplation make us better men?"

"Yes, automatically! But never in comparison with others. Proper spiritual growth is not in a specific cult. It is in the heart of the Being. Moreover, do not think that all your wishes will come true by doing these spiritual exercises, for that will not be the case — Meditation and Contemplation help us create a bridge between our wishful thinking personalities and our True Self."

"Thank you for the explanation."

"The gratitude is all mine."

After saying goodbye, the two men disappeared into the insistent cold of the night. Then silence invaded the space, letting the fog completely cover Samah's view.

---

[3] "HU will put a fresh, new spirit into your life. You will begin to be a happier person, because It will show you what things are truly important for you and what are not." — Harold Klemp, The Awakening Soul, p. 66

In the heart of the kind-hearted extends the spacious garden of life. This is where the fragrant flowers of Genuine Beauty sing the melodies of self-love and love for others.

The dance of the stars

One evening, while Haroldo was contemplating at the foot of Samah, most of the peasants were gathered in the village's courtyard to chat. Eduardo also took part in that joyful moment that comforted everyone's heart. At the end of the recreation, he took the road back home. At some point, he spotted the master, who was sitting cross-legged. With his eyes closed, he was chanting HU. Not far away from him was Pipa, Kunda's most beloved dog. The seeker joined them without thinking.

Although Haroldo seemed relatively young, his manner was like that of wise older men. His calmness in speaking and his patience in listening awakened Eduardo's curiosity, that had once nourished him in his grandfather's tales.

Seeing certain temperance through the master's stillness, the disciple could not contain himself with silence. He wanted to get his attention somehow. So he let out a sigh so delicate that the voice of the silence of that landscape seemed to speak louder.

However, the master's senses were very sharp. He opened his eyes gently, smiled at the disciple, and closed his eyes again. Although he did not participate in the joyful gathering of the peasants, he was also happy. His smile made Eduardo realize that one can find joy in the most contemplative moment. After this internal reflection, the seeker, too, expressed a smile at the corner of his lips and said, "Before I arrived here, I stood for a moment watching you, and suddenly I noticed a grain of wisdom in your silence. Can this be considered a virtue?"

Pipa, satisfied with her food, was lying on the ground without any anxiety, waiting for rest to come. Anyone there could witness the dog's quietness. Haroldo reopened his eyes, observed the animal for a moment, and answered, "There is no virtue without Love and no love without virtue, for Love, in other words, is the essence of all virtue."

"If I understand correctly, can one say that all virtue begins in Love?"

"Exactly! An intelligence that serves to manipulate or corrupt does not cease to be intelligence. However, it will never be a virtue. Virtues serve to take the man out of the clutches of ephemeral pleasures. Therefore, whatever you do, do it with Love, and you will practice virtues. In this way, you will be a free being."

The two men remained silent. Although Haroldo was deeply engaged in contemplation, he was fully aware of the questions that resonated in the disciple's heart. At some point, he said, "Eduardo, I feel that there is another question in your heart. You may speak."

The seeker was astonished to realize that the master could see what was inside him. He had already learned that Contemplation and Meditation allow the soul to see things that the body could never perceive. After this consideration, he began to speak, "A few months ago, you told me about your encounter with Reba, the august master. Sometimes I wonder if you have ever met this majestic being again."

"Yes, I am one with Reba, just as you are one with me. Together with Reba, we are united until the end of time. The truth is that all beings, animate or not, are bound by ties that were never woven."

Eduardo frowned, for he could not grasp the depth of what the master was saying. Always smiling, the master continued, "The tremendous universal web lines are imperceptible to those who do not look and do not listen with the heart. But I tell you, my son, although the ties that bind us are invisible, they will never be corrupted."

"I see only dimly the meaning of your words."

"One day, when you tire the eyes, you will see with your heart, and the truth will be revealed to you."

"I hope very much that this day is near."

"There is always a time for everything in life. Be patient. Your sun will shine one day or another."

Eduardo shook his head as if he agreed with his master. Then a sign of credulity showed on his face. He knew that the master was right, but deep inside, he felt that he was not yet ready to see the true colors of the universe. Fortunately, the master had already taught him how to deal with the tricks of the mind. At that moment, he was very aware of what was happening inside and outside of him. Through Mindfulness, Intelligence, and Attention, he realized that this sudden disbelief about his success on the path to self-realization was one of the many ways the mind corrupts the soul's dreams and aspirations. With inner contemplation, he remembered when the master told him that only the heart's strength lifts mountains. Then he asked himself, "Does the mountain represent our fears and limitations?"

His ignorance led him to sabotage his greatest desire, the burning desire to know the truth of the heart. When he saw how his undisciplined mind was playing, he laughed quietly and briefly. Then he said goodbye to the master.

Haroldo returned to his internal contemplation. The dog Pipa came closer to him, and it seemed that only the brightness of the master could give her the warmth she needed on that cold night.

Eduardo continued on his way, heading for the house. After a few steps ahead, he stopped and looked back. There was Samah, the imposing mountain that seemed to make its way through the dark but luminous firmament.

The twinkling stars had placed themselves high above Samah to shine brightly in the deep pool of sky. They seemed to celebrate the mountain. Though these stars were inert, their brightness was like a dance, a celestial dance. It was a delight that caused rejoicing in the hearts of those who walked the road of LOVE.

This vision amazed the seeker's heart. Witnessing this unique ceremony that only the soul can contemplate, Eduardo remembered one of the Southlands inhabitants. This man had told him that it was indeed possible to touch heaven while being here on earth. That night, Eduardo had just touched the sky and the stars with only his eyes.

The marks

That morning was exceptional. For the first time in many years, Eduardo woke up, amazed by the beauty of life. He left the house, singing the praises of the Creator. On the way to the field, he enthusiastically admired the perfection of nature, and after a thousand steps of singing, he exclaimed, "What a splendid day!"

Just like the soldier who longs to see his family again after many years, the seeker could not stop thinking about the endless list of questions he would ask his master in the evening. Soon after leaving the camp, he headed for Haroldo's abode with an exhausted body and sharp lips. There was his master waiting for him.

"Good evening, master."

 "Good evening."

Eduardo wasted no time and began to speak, "There are so many things that surprise me about life, but one thing especially puzzles me."

"What is it?"

"I am talking about man's capacity to endure pain. Sometimes I see him being dragged along by the burden of life, and I look at him and ask him, 'Are you all right?' He answers, 'I am fine'. In some cases, I offer him my help, but he looks at me with a timid face and says, 'Everything will be fine.' The most surprising thing of all is when I see myself behaving precisely like this.

"What do you mean?"

"In truth, I am used to saying that everything is fine when it is not. Deep in my heart, I carry the conflict of sincerity. Some say that man has no limits, that he can do anything, and I believe them. So I close my eyes and pretend that life is not being tricky with me. I live in vain, hoping that one day the future will be kinder."

After a moment, Eduardo, his face afflicted, looked insistently at the master and continued, "When I see the sea of sorrows submerge the most pleasant aspects of the world, I think all existence boils down to suffering. In childhood, people used to tell me, 'Think and be,' and since then, I have not stopped thinking, but I have never come TO BE[4]. When I stand in front of the mirror, I cannot recognize my interlocutor. Life has marked me. Yet, I am still walking. Misfortunes never stop chasing me. And when I solve one, I take a breath, and there is another one waiting for me. There are no more days of quiet in this world. Everywhere men cause wars, calling for peace, and all that is left there is desolation. What can we say to those who love life while it seems to conspire against them? The desire to fly away from all of this is immense, but I look back and realize that I do not have wings. What to do? Many false prophets promise us a better life. Does tranquility exist in this world? Can I believe in the happiness I see through the eyes of Kunda's peasants?"

"Don't you remember any good moments in life?"

"I remember my lovely childhood moments. Yet, the human condition is something I do not understand. Deep down, I want to see people free themselves from the fears that plague them."

"How can you demand from the world what it does not have? Have you ever wondered about it? How can your neighbor give you love if he does not know it himself?"

"I had never thought of it this way."

"We can only give that which already exists within us. If the world has no more love to provide you, then be the gift of love for it. Give what you wish to receive. If you want love, then give love. If you want peace, then offer your peaceful companionship to

---

[4] TO BE here means to become a Self-realized Person.

whoever is next to you. The vanity of unrighteous men can never be a burden to you, for your heart is light, your steps are fleeting, and your shadow is impossible to grasp. Amid the chaos, you must confront the winds of uncertainty to let the breeze of hope spring up in your core, without fear of the unknown. Always remember that happiness is not in things or people. It is within you. Prosperity may not have arrived yet but have freedom in your heart and never turn away from Love. If you do not want to be your sadness tomorrow, be your happiness today because what you become tomorrow reflects what you are today. Life is pure justice. Now, go home, my son. Take a sweet bath. Try to empty your mind, and be grateful with the night, so that the dawn will be kind to you. Also, as soon as you wake up, come directly to me, and we will discuss together the Justice of Life."

"Thank you very much, master."

"The gratitude is all mine."

A prince with no kingdom

Eduardo started the day in happiness, but he was steeped in sadness by the time evening came. He had remonstrated a lot about the pains of humanity while he was talking with his master. He could not let go of the pain.

Even though he genuinely wanted to give to the world what was already in short supply, the injustices of men still plagued him. He felt minuscule and unable to provide the love that humanity essentially needed. He thought, "Why can't I feel the Unity anymore, as I did in the episode with the old Bokô? Why so many ups and downs? Why do I complain so much about the order of things? Am I not yet ready to see the answers?"

He arrived home dismayed. He took a bath and tried to empty his mind as the master had recommended. In an unsuccessful attempt to silence his thoughts, he decided to do some contemplation. He sat cross-legged at the head of the bed and tried unsuccessfully to quiet his mind, but it kept stirring his thoughts.

This made him begin to chant a mantra. "What better mantra than the name of the Supreme?" he asked himself. Then he began to contemplate, chanting, "Hu-u-u-u-u-u-u-u-u," silently and repetitively until he fell asleep and dreamed.

That morning had come as a new promise. The seeker seemed less shaken by what had happened the day before. The serene smile on his face implied that last night had fulfilled the promises Haroldo had made to him. He arrived, greeting the master with great joy.

"Good morning", said Eduardo.

The master, as always, was waiting in front of his abode.

"I am fine, how are you? Seeing the splendor of your face, I can imagine that the stars of the night have revealed themselves to you. How was your sleep?" asked the master.

"The thoughts were jumping around in my tormented mind. I questioned, a bit confused, and discouraged by not understanding the Divine flow. While awake, I did not have the clarity to observe the night, as I felt mentally exhausted and a tightness in my chest. Only with HU could I sleep and to my delight, I dreamed. This dream was indeed enlightening and answered the questions I had asked myself before going to sleep. Now I am amazed that I can see life differently, just as you wish. For the first time, I witnessed the sweetness of the night and saw something in it that I had never seen before."

"What did you see?"

"Night has let down its guard, and through its dark curtain, I have been able to contemplate life quite clearly. Today, I am a new man with a different vision. In the Southlands, they say that the blind man who regains his sight has a habit of exchanging mountains for hills and hills for plains. I must admit that after tonight I internally see mountains instead of hills and hills instead of plains. However, I am convinced that my new vision is one of the thousand facets of Genuine Justice," explained Eduardo.

"In the world, what seems constant is never permanent. Yesterday, I saw you complain of injustice, and today I see you proud of Divine Justice. Life is designed by cycles, and there is no eternal suffering. Now, tell me how your night went."

"Master, I have dreamed of a past life. It brought me the truth to free me from the affliction that I stored in my heart for a long time. I dreamed that I was a rich, handsome, fortunate man. I dreamed that the world around me bowed in reverence every time I passed by. I dreamed that I was the king's son and that everything I desired soon belonged to me. I dreamed that the ease of life had made me arrogant with my servants and cheeky with my family members. I dreamed that I fell in love with a servant girl named Diva. My family being royalty would never let me marry a servant. All suffering in that existence was the fault of noble blood, the same blood that gifted me all the freedoms of life only to take away later the true freedom — that of love. I learned to speak like a king, to philosophize like an aristocrat, and to command men like an emperor. In that part of the world, no one knew more about rhetoric than I did, yet even then, I could not convince my parents of the heart's reasons. Blessed with the good things in life but devoid of love, I then became a rebel of rules and morals. My rebellion caused outrage to my noble parents. Forbidden to love a servant, I deserted my palace and became a prince without a kingdom. Despite all the morals I was taught, I deliberately trod the path of depravity, opulence, and disorder. Suddenly, one lonely afternoon, vice came to me and convinced me of its friendship. Soon, I drowned all my sorrow in the most expensive wine in town. Counselors and doctors did not cure my depression. Unconcerned about life, I persisted in drinking wine until the day my heart overflowed with it, and thus all the blood in my body became wine. I spent months drinking and regurgitating until the day my voice left me. Finally, on a night like any other, sitting thoughtfully on the sofa, I heard the angel of death knock on my door. I opened it, but being mute, I could not tell him that I was not yet ready to leave. That is how the dream came to an end."

"It seems that sadness follows you in your dreams."

"No, master, my affliction is over. I feel free from the past."

"Did you realize that when understanding comes, suffering ends?"

"Yes, that is what happened to me."

"What was your understanding then?"

"Last night's dream seemed as natural to me as our conversations. After I woke up, I started to think. At that moment, the relation between that vision and my present life became evident. I understood why I hate wine so much today. The more I think about it all; I realize that the present life has taken away all my freedoms except 'love'. Today, I am not fortunate, I am not rich, I am not the son of a king, and I am not powerful. However, in my veins flows the compassion of ten thousand men and, despite the sorrows of life, I remain as loving as ever, for to love is what I do best. I no longer doubt that being able to love is far more rewarding than being born a prince. For all these years, I've been complaining about my existence. I got used to seeing evil in all aspects of daily life, but now I realize that all these torments have made me a loving man. Today, I no longer deny my suffering, but the truth is that I am a much happier man than a prince rejected by his people. Moreover, I better understand my deep gratitude for my parents. In the present life, I did not need private lessons in philosophy and rhetoric to know that a child should honor his parents. In the dream, I was an ungrateful man for owning many things. Today I am grateful that I possess only myself. The vision made me realize that it is much more valuable to possess oneself than to possess the things of this world. After all, what is the point of having gold without knowing how to use it? But it took a small death of mine to see life in this way. A part of me, the illusion, the ego, had to die. Usually for us humans, death is not one of the easiest passages. I was afraid to let myself die. I understand this now. That is why I suffered. I do not know yet how ready I am, but from now on I will follow the path of love courageously. Master, this is my understanding."

"Such is the happiness I feel now, for to witness the spiritual rebirth of a man is a blessing. I can say with certainty that you have become a changed man. From now on, you will see the world in other colors. I am deeply grateful to witness this."

The two men observed a moment of silence. Suddenly, the seeker remembered that they had not yet had breakfast. With a smile on his lips, he said, "Master, perhaps it would be wise for us to have breakfast to continue our conversation better."

"How wonderful. Let's go, then."

The two men entered Haroldo's house.

All the perfection of the world, all the grandeur of the universe, all the plurality of life, all the infinitude of the cosmos, all this is nothing but the Soul manifesting itself.

Time

Existence in the village moved smoothly. When experiencing life in the capitals, it is challenging to ignore time. That day, after his toil, the seeker sat in front of the Sita River. For hours, he was thoughtful, wondering why the days in Kunda went so slowly.

Before him, there was Sita, which was flowing smoothly. Not only was the current gentle, but it seemed it had always been this way. Observing the moderate dance of the water, the seeker asked himself, "All my life, I have watched men running after time. What madness has condemned them to run so fast?"

Suddenly, he heard Haroldo's voice saying, "Sooner or later, the river will flow into the sea." Eduardo was already used to the master's sudden appearances. He did not waste time and started talking, "Today, I observed nature for hours. I looked at the trees and noticed in their silence, the smile of gratitude. I looked at the sky, and mysteriously, my ears began to tune in to the festival of birds. I looked at the ground and encountered the pilgrimage of the ants. All this reminded me of devotion. When I lifted my head, I witnessed the spectacle of the river. Beauty has always been beside me, and I, like a madman, had never looked at it. For all these years, I have never been able to contemplate the exquisiteness of nature. But why does this happen to me?"

"Because man chases time without ever reaching it, which led him to put a price on it. Since then, he runs after it, never resting. Here in the village of Kunda, men are content with the little they have. This reality makes time to spare so that they can taste the delights of heaven. Isn't it beautiful to see?"

"It is more than beautiful," said Eduardo, enchanted by the colors of the horizon.

The master did not respond. However, he looked at his disciple with love, and left, taking with him the sound emanating from the landscape. Without moving, the disciple kept his gaze fixed on Sita's dance. The serenity on his face revealed his satisfaction with the master's teachings.

The Gift

The following day, the seeker woke up suspiciously. Looking at the sun that was late to rise, he knew that something was missing in nature. He sensed that something was wrong but could not determine what it was. His mind kept churning out thoughts — question after question until the calmness faded away.

After his toil, he took his coat and went to meet his master. When he arrived at the foot of the mountain, he found him sitting serenely as always.

"Good evening, master."

"Good evening, everything, all right?"

"Not very well. I am worried about everything around me. It seems that nature is different today. I have the feeling that something is missing. However, my conviction tells me that this situation is yet to come. It seems that I am worried about the future."

"Past and future are only measures of the present. If you pay attention to only one of them, you will lose your proper measure. What you should do is to live fully in the eternal present."

"Can you tell me more in detail?"

"Through awareness of the Now, you unravel the secrets of the past and the mystery of the future. In this way, you build a bright future for yourself. It is up to you to comprehend what is happening in the present moment. Do you understand?"

"More or less."

"Now, tell me, what is the present moment telling you?"

"When I think about the present, I feel tranquility, like I felt yesterday, by the river. But this serenity is not lasting today. I am already thinking of what I will do without you, and this torments me. How can I face life without your advice?"

"The day when I will say goodbye to Samah, will come soon."

"O master, will you abandon me? Without you, I am nothing. How will I live?"

"Cycles make life. The physical worlds are subject to change, and this is inevitable. For all things in this world, there is a beginning and an end. Human existence bears witness to this reality."

"I cannot see myself without you guiding me. There is still so much to know, so much to learn."

"Without me, you have traveled the world, you have known many cultures, you have become a better and worthy man. Does none of this count for you?"

"Yes, it does, but I like more the one I became since I met you."

"You greatly underestimate yourself. Avoid this. Know that everything you have done up to now, is part of your formation. That every detail of your history, prepared you to be who you are, and brought you here. It would be best if you were grateful for that."

"All my gratitude praises you. You made me see the light amid the darkness. Today, I can easily observe the greed of the mind. I owe all my greatness to you, and I want you to know that," said Eduardo.

"They say that one must be prepared to behold the splendor of the Magnificent. Otherwise, you can lose sight. This is a good analogy for the relationship of the master-disciple. The genuine Master appears when the disciple is ready. You have not come to me; I have come to you. Like the breeze that touches the face without ever getting attached, I will leave the same way I arrived. The Master's job is to show the disciple the path to wisdom. However, it is the disciple himself who begins the journey. Do not forget that the search for wisdom does not walk outside, but inside the Being. Now that you know where your true home is, you must return to the realm of unworthy men to raise the human consciousness."

"My people are highly materialistic. They will not listen to me. I do not know where my relatives are. Everything there seems lost to me. They say that worldly life brings tyranny to the people, making the wishes of the wicked the law that subjugates the innocent. In the Central Lands, injustice has become the majority's voice, and I cannot take a risk putting myself in this chaos."

"What your people need is what you can give them. It is what you have inside you," murmured the master.

"What else do I have to give except love? My people do not know what love is anymore. What about the foreigners there? My people no longer know how to love what appears to be different. How can I change this consciousness?"

"Every good man has the heart of a king. As a man who knows nothing but love, you will love your people. As a king who was once a seeker in foreign lands, you will become a good ruler for foreigners. Now, I must go. I have to take care of some things," responded Haroldo.

"Thank you, master."

The two men disappeared, letting inertia invade the space. Quiescence covered the landscape around Kunda. The stars in the dark sky shone brightly above Samah. The night was beautiful.

Seven Days

For the next three days, Haroldo was gone. His absence in Kunda was not usual. Eduardo walked around thoughtfully, wondering where his master was. He still wondered what he would do without his guide around. Inside the restless man, grief conquered his thoughts, and torment became absolute. The seeker, as always, needed answers. At various times, he tried to meditate without success, for his thoughts lost observation. Although he had already received the master's teachings on dealing with fear, he could not stop dreading the reality of having to face life without his master by his side.

Another four days added up to the agony of waiting. Seven days went by without Samah's friend's appearance, but this did not change the peasants' routine. They did not even notice the master's absence. They moved from one corner to another in search of their own business. It was harvest week. For the peasants, the harvest is the best phase of their toil. There is nothing more rewarding than enjoying the fruits of their labor. This is when the hand that once tore from cutting the grass receives in its palm the justice that is due to it. The peasants were grateful before nature. Around Samah, happiness had spread to everyone except Eduardo.

The disciple retreated to his host's house, permanently pondering about the uncertainty of the future. He was even the only farmer in the village not to harvest the fruit of his labor. It was seven days of mental agony, and just as he was thinking of resigning himself to the absence of his master, he heard a familiar voice speaking, "They say that the future enchants in good faith, yet it never responds to our wishes. Whenever we ardently desire it, it is never willingly given to us, and when we give up believing, a light appears at the end of the tunnel. Yet we do not see it, for he who has no faith sees nothing."

"O master, you have abandoned me. I spent seven days in the most profound anguish, and suddenly, you appeared talking about the future. The truth is that I cannot see my future without your presence. It kills me with sadness even when everything around me sprinkles drops of happiness. During the entire week of the harvest, I saw my thoughts chattering, and when I realized what was happening to me, I perceived that there was in all my thoughts the old and well-known fear of facing life alone," said Eduardo, sadly.

"I cannot believe that the man who has traveled the world alone is afraid to face it today. I thought our conversations had prepared you to accept the universe in its proper form."

"I went out into the world ignoring its truths. Today I am a changed man, and I will certainly think twice before exploring the earth's roads again."

"Do you think that you would be who you are today if you had not traveled the world the way you did?"

"I cannot answer that, but it seems that my travels have led me to you."

"Our meeting was the answer to an equation, which we failed to answer more than a thousand years ago. Remember that nothing comes suddenly. Greed has made man believe in chance, which does not exist. The foundation of the physical world comes down to the Law of Cause and Effect. Along with this comes the Law of Duality, and thus other laws follow. As long as men live under the sun, they are bound to be subject to these laws."

"How to understand the meaning of Life?", asked Eduardo.

"Live more in the 'Now'. That is enough to grasp the meaning of Life."

"Master, what can I do to understand better these laws that govern the world?"

"The Laws of the world are contemplated through the consciousness of the present moment, in the Now. If you want to live for real, be aware of what you do in your daily life. Contemplate the things around you and, above all, meditate on life outside and inside of you. At every moment, something beautiful is happening, something divine, something spectacular, something rejuvenating, something that makes us fall in love with existence and its wonders. All we need is the eyes to notice this reality. Unfortunately, our problem is that we are so preoccupied with the past and the future that we do not see Life in its entirety. This was your case. You spent seven days in agony and fear of finding yourself alone in the face of Life. You failed to live these last days properly because of something you could not control."

"Yes, that is true. I confess that it was a bit selfish of me to think mainly about what I would do without you, but I was also very concerned about you. I felt that some harm had come to you."

"This wonderful week of harvest brought joy and happiness to life around the mountain, but you chose to put yourself outside of it all, under the pretext of an uncertain future. You missed the opportunity to savor the happiness of the present moment. The 'present' is a gift. Why waste it?"

"A few months ago, we talked about the attachment that breeds fear. At the time, it seemed to me that I could already override my mind. Now I am disappointed to realize that I still have a long way to go to reach Myself. The way home is longer and narrower than I imagined."

"Reaching the top of the mountain does not guarantee achievement. At any moment, you can fall again, and if you do not, the hill can collapse. This is precisely why Intelligence, Attention, and Mindfulness can never be left aside," said Haroldo.

"Master, months ago, you have said something like, 'only those who are on the top of the mountain will know eternal rest,' but now you said the opposite. I know there was no confusion on your part, so could you tell me more about it?"

"When I said, 'only he who is on the top of the mountain will know eternal rest,' I was not referring to a goal, not even to the mountain Samah. We all have a particular and irregular mountain to climb every day. And mine will never be the same as yours. I believe that the goal of the Soul is the ultimate encounter with the Supreme. But the Love of the Creator did not bring us here to fulfill a purpose. It wants us to enjoy the ascent back to Its abode. But each of us has his path to follow, neither better nor worse, but unique. And on this path, there may be a series of slippery obstacles that will make us fall. But those who trust in something greater than materialistic illusion keep going. When I say, 'Reaching the top of the mountain does not guarantee fulfillment,' it is so that you do not rush to get somewhere. The complete realization of Being is inevitable. There is no denying or disputing the inescapable. You will reach the top naturally by Being a Soul. Many people, wishing to accelerate their process, do everything, do dozens of 'so-called spiritual' procedures to get there and receive enlightenment. But do you see that this brings us back to the subject of Attachment?"

"Yes," answered Eduardo.

"Do not get attached to the result. Do not get attached to the top. Appreciate the path. Appreciate everything about it, including the slips due to the uneven terrain. Life was made for you to look at each moment as unique, both in its joys and its sorrows."

Haroldo remained silent for a moment and finally continued, "Changing the subject, it was seven anxious days for you. As for me, it was seven days of pilgrimage. In view of such a situation, I think we both need a good rest."

"I need to rest my mind."

"Go home now and come back tomorrow. I will be waiting for you right here, at the foot of the mountain."

After thanking the master, the disciple took the road back to his host's house. Deep in his heart, he knew that the farewell with Samah's friend had come. Fortunately, due to that day's teachings, the fear in his mind was gone. With his new clarity, he felt able to deal with the future. What mattered most to him was the present moment, and that moment was resting the mind. Only the stillness of the spirit could bring him more tranquility after seven days of torment. He arrived at home and hurriedly went to bed.

The sermon

The following day, Eduardo went to the foot of the mountain to wait for his master. He was aware of the farewell that was about to take place. The seeker stopped lamenting and complaining. He observed life around him and soon realized that, that morning, there was nothing different in nature. Everything was in its proper place. He sat down at the foot of Samah, from where he could contemplate the happiness that the last seven days had brought to the peasants of Kunda. There he said to himself, "I cannot believe I traded the happiness of seven days for the torments of the spirit. Not even a donkey would do such a thing."

At that moment, Haroldo appeared. Soon, after greeting him, the seeker began to speak, "Master, when I think about everything I have seen during my travels, I realize that division is the evil of humanity. To perpetuate this viciousness in the world, human beings had to adopt a specific way of thinking. Thus, the conditioned man was born. He thinks, acts, believes, and disbelieves according to what society taught him. This person cannot perceive his condition as a mental slave. Man is convinced by his vanity. He is not certain, but believes he knows the Supreme Creator. Then, he goes from the greed of words to the death of the spirit. From there, the same man tries to prove that the Unmanifest does not exist. It is like denying the verb's existence, using other verbs in the defense thesis. I need to see, understand, and know. Please tell me about men and the Supreme, because everything I see in this world leaves me confused. Sometimes I find myself disoriented, and I know I should not be like this. You previously told me that cycles make the waves of life's sea, and that change is the only thing that remains unchangeable. Today a man is born, tomorrow he dies. One day, he is happy; another day, he is sad. But in the end, you have to lose yourself to find your true self."

"I see a pinch of wisdom in your words. It makes me happy," murmured Haroldo.

"Being here today at the foot of the mountain, I can feel the grandeur and splendor of nature. There is no confusion in what I can see. I have noticed that beauty is always justice. But one thing is to perceive, another is to feel."

"Have you wondered about the fate of humanity?" asked Haroldo.

"I have no clear idea, but I am convinced that humanity will not stop until it reaches Love."

"Now, what can you say about man?"

"It is hard to comprehend the human being. Today he is generous. Tomorrow, he is greedy. Through vanity, he makes his own words the 'words of the Supreme.' I know that the Giant Soul of the world speaks to man, but I also know that man speaks for himself. With propriety, he shouts the names of the Supreme from every corner. He has not yet understood that perhaps it is impolite to call the name of the one he does not know. My veneration for that which does not manifest itself is profound, so I am careful not to call It in vain. Seeing things this way, how can one interpret the concept of the unmanifest?"

"Eduardo, if you count on your eyes to see the unseen, you will see nothing. If you depend on your mind to know the unknowable, you will know nothing. And if you count on your hands to touch the untouchable, you will grasp nothing. All things will abandon the man who pursues the Sacred in the things of this world. However, after having left the things of this world, he who surrenders himself to the Sacred will become master of himself and all things. How can one understand the One who does not manifest Himself? How can one listen to the One that no words can describe?"

"What other path than that of search can lead us to the Supreme Truth? If I attempt to touch It, It will escape me. What should I do in such a situation?"

"The man who ardently desires something desires it out of passion, and by his thoughts, he will become a prisoner of himself. Thus, his vision will never be sharp enough to see the light of contentment. Now, tell me, how can the prodigal son remember his father while ignoring his family name?"

"It will be challenging for him, for the family name reminds him of the origin, the source from which he came. In other words, the son must know himself, and thus he will see the father."

"Eduardo, from now on, listen to me carefully. What I am about to say is my sermon about life. Before I begin, I ask forgiveness from the intelligence that governs the universe because audacity has led man to speak of what he does not know. Today I dawned singing HU, one of the thousand names of the Absolute Soul. My sermon knows the truth, for the words come from the heart. But deep down, I am only a messenger, and I am aware of worldly terms' limitations. Once, on a deserted night, a man found himself alone in front of his affliction. He had already blamed life and his neighbor. At that moment, he was about to condemn death, but how to judge the mystery? Suddenly, he heard the cry of silence. It was absolute silence. Not even the voice of a thousand men would shout so loudly. The Ultimate Light came to the door of the solitary man and knocked with consistency. The man had to open it, for the one awaiting him on the other side was none other than Himself. The immensity of Being was within his grasp. When he reaches his true home, he will see with the eyes of his heart the golden face of the One who has loved him since even before eternity. If you ask me what eternity is, I will answer you that it is that which does not count days, nor nights. It is that which recognizes no forms, no movements. Whoever ventures to know eternity must first realize that life and death return to the same source. For in the world of worlds, everything is real, and nothing is transformed or created. However, in the land of illusion, when everything ceases to be, nothing comes up. In a beautiful instant, the seeker of the Genuine Truth will reach the consciousness of Unity, where there is no division, where the Being is everything and nothing. Then he will realize that only in illusory worlds are things created or transformed because, in the World of worlds, the Truth remains."

On the seeker's lips was a smile of contentment. He listened with love, and through this marvelous feeling, he had established himself in the now, in that exact moment when the master was speaking to him about the design of existence. He looked in wonder at the master and savored his sayings with a delight that was unparalleled in the world. He then surrendered to the wisdom that echoed in the fragrant breeze that surrounded them.

With his eyes fixed on the disciple, the master continued, "Remember. All the earth's paths lead to the Supreme Creator, but only the heart's route will touch the light of a thousand suns. Do not trivialize my words and listen thoughtfully. When the vain one learns to let go of this world's things, what is essential will be given to him. Power will become a simple tool for Love. Power will be nothing more than this, for man will have already gone beyond passions and, therefore, desires. Where does the blind man who entrusts his sight to another blind man want to go? Beware of people who say that you are what you think you are. They are not themselves when they say such a thing. Be master of your thoughts, and make your mind serve Love. The Genuine Being is beyond ideas. It is what you feel at your core. Remember that I love you, a love that words cannot measure. How to use the temporal to evaluate the timeless? Distance is nothing before the loving heart. I have been, am, and will always be with you. Keep me in your heart, and do not judge the strangers or those dear to you. Quiet your thoughts, contemplate, meditate, and lovingly chant HU, one of the names of the Supreme Creator. Then life itself will reveal the road of spiritual freedom to you through the heart that loves. I wanted to convey that message to you. Before me, many have said that. After me, others will say it. But, one thing is to believe, another is to witness the moment when faith consolidates itself through the experience."

"Some men I know would never believe your sermon. What would you say to them?"

"Before human insanity, the only thing left to us is to dream in the Political Ideal and live that Ideal in our daily lives. There is harmony in the experience of those whose eyes see Justice, Beauty, Kindness, and Gratitude in all things."

"Master, your sermon seems like a farewell. But, for the first time, I feel serenity in knowing that you are leaving, and I no longer question whether you will ever return. Under your wings, I have learned that detachment frees us from fear and, therefore, from torment. Today I can be content with the happiness of the present moment. I am happy now."

"Eduardo, I am leaving."

"Master, despite my happiness, I must remind you that you have spoken a lot about the Supreme Creator, but you have not said what It is."

"No one could tell you what the Supreme is except yourself. Find yourself and explore your relationship with the Absolute Father."

"They say that there was Oneness even before creation. So I ask myself, 'Who am I? Am I the Oneness? If so, why do I feel like a being apart as I walk the Earth's paths? Despite the oblivion, my heart believes that I know the heaven that seems far away from men. Master, if everything was of the same essence, if, before the beginning of time, there was the Unity, and if it is perfect and complete by itself, why then did multiplicity manifest itself?"

"Son, what would the sea be without the rivers if the sea is already abundance?" asked the master.

Eduardo thought for a while, and after expressing a rejuvenating smile, he said with the most remarkable gentleness, "Only the river that consciously flows to join the sea will find the answer, for then it will have become the sea itself.[5]"

"The Supreme is all things, and within them remains the Unity, unchangeable, eternally equal to Itself. Look, my son, the Oneness is what you will recognize when you open the door of your heart," said the master.

Astonished, the seeker preferred a word to silence. With the palms of his two hands joined at the level of his heart, and with a movement of his head that seemed to revere the Augustus, the disciple softly responded, "Thank you, master." With those words, the men said goodbye, which they did by simultaneously uttering, "To our reunions!"

The rain began to fall. For a few moments, Eduardo enjoyed the drops that touched his face and then took care to find a shelter to admire the water that fell like a blessing from the Lord of Creation. With a serene expression on his lips, he stood at the foot of Samah, looking at his master, who was walking away. Haroldo, all wet, did not seem to mind the legion of drops that stroked his head with little gray hair.

In that moment of inner peace, the seeker knew that the next day would be ideal for climbing to the top of the mountain, which he had already tried a few times without success. He knew that the master had been at the top of Samah many times. One day, he had come to Haroldo and asked the secret of this feat. In reply, the master had said, "Only the strength of the heart can lift mountains." Eduardo never understood the phrase's meaning, but now he was confident about the climbing. He kept in his heart the words spoken by the master about not getting attached to the climb's goal. The seeker now understood the mountain's representation in his life and knew that even if he reached the top of Samah, he would continue climbing his inner mountain, getting to know himself each new day. Thanks to the teachings, he was more prepared for this.

---

[5] Inspired by "The Prophet" of Kahlil Gibran.

The adult asked the little girl, "What do you want to be when you grow up?"
The little girl, confused, answered, "What do you mean? I already AM!"

Self-realization

That night was beautiful. Eduardo surrendered to deep serenity, where the mind has no dominion, where thoughts do not exist, where silence and emptiness become one. It was a solemn sleep, a sleep of a thousand dreams and, at the same time, of none. He had never experienced such stillness until that night. This sensation was new. So soon after waking, he asked himself, "Is this what it feels like to awaken without having desires?"

For many years, he had been crossing continents in search of answers. There was not a night when he did not long for the face of the Absolute Father. Likewise, there had been several mornings when he had been frustrated not to possess what he had ardently desired. But the night before, it was different. After the master had left, no resentment remained in the disciple's heart.

Eduardo might not understand many things, but of one thing he knew — dancing. As is known, he who dances to the rhythm of life understands that comings and goings are nothing before the immensity that exists far beyond space and time.

In the past, he had experienced some disappointments when trying to climb the mountain. But now, he was about to overcome his boundaries. That morning would be the first of many successful adventures in a new perspective of life.

Eduardo then went to climb the trail. They were three days of pilgrimage, three days of complete contentment and appreciation, three days that passed as quickly as a shooting star. During his journey, he was an enemy of thoughts, and a profound silence accompanied him until he reached the top of the mountain Samah.

Standing on the mountaintop looking out over the vastness of the universe around him, the seeker, who had been searching for the truth for many lifetimes, found his answer the moment he stopped searching, the moment he stood in silence to observe the light and listen to the voice of the unmanifest.

With a radiant smile, the man thought to himself, "I have traveled from world to world, from West to East, from North to South. All this to finally find peace at the top of a mountain in the Central Lands. Yesterday, I stood at the foot of Samah and believed in the beauty there. Standing now at its summit, I realize that there are no words to describe Genuine Beauty. Whoever said that it is possible to measure eternity has lied to himself. Therefore, I lack the words to say what I see at this very moment."

After a short silence, followed by an internal Contemplation. The seeker expressed in words his heartfelt:

O Giant Soul, Soul of all souls
Before You, I feel paralyzed
by the duality of the senses.

O Beloved Father,
show me the Path of paths,
teach me selflessness and bravery,
illuminate my steps on the path of the heart.

For millions of years, I have wandered
But now, I know You love me

At that point in space, words were scarce, but so was life-sustaining air. Suddenly Eduardo lost consciousness. He found himself in an unknown place, beyond all imagination. He could not differentiate reality from his dream, nor could he identify or perceive his body. All he could feel was the fluctuation of his consciousness. It was certainly the perception of an unnamable sensation or something that was beyond body and mind. He could perceive the air's movement, and the glowing green of nature seemed to be older than the earth of men. The feeling of peace was total, and the seeker repeatedly asked himself if this was the realm of the Supreme Creator.

Floating above and below the grayish clouds, he could feel some unknown energy. This sensation was neither cold nor hot, yet it made him feel cold and warm at the same time. He experienced his communion with the universal consciousness. At the same time, he felt like a particle. For in a moment, he was everything. In another, he was nothing. There was no measure of proportion because one moment he felt more prominent than the world, and the next he felt smaller than a grain of sand. There was no space or time; everything fits together harmoniously. With that expansion of consciousness and the veil of ignorance stripped away, the seeker could perceive the totality of the universe.

Surrounding his heavenly body floating from cloud to cloud were two beings who witnessed the whole scene. They had a human appearance, yet they were luminous figures. Instantly, the seeker recognized his master Haroldo. Then he wondered who the second being was. Suddenly he remembered the beautiful twilights when he sat next to his master to honor the guardians of the Golden Wisdom Temples. Thus, he recognized the mysterious messenger. "That must be the Majestic Reba," thought the seeker.

Without saying anything, he just glanced at his master. At that moment, he foresaw the answers to all his questions and soon understood that there is no question without a previous response. His master had already said that the voice of silence shines brighter than a thousand fires. He realized that nothing could separate him from Haroldo. He knew that death and life are the same and that everything is Unity. He noticed that no entity creates or transforms anything under the Heaven of the heavens. As a conscious observer, he concluded that there is no difference between the totality and the no-thing. They are of the same essence, all part of the Supreme Unity.

Together with the two other beings, the seeker found himself in front of a golden temple on top of a mountain. When he arrived there, he saw a splendid book in the distance, which seemed more extensive than the whole universe. But as he got closer to it, the book got smaller and smaller until it fit in his tactless hands. The lightness of the book amazed him.

Neither of the two beings accompanying him tried to stop him from opening it, yet in the depths of his being, he knew he was not yet ready to read it. So he returned the book to its origin, and with the silence of a thousand words, the three beings flew away.

There was a vibration in the air that intermingled with an explosion of a thousand voices. At the same time, the symphony present in that void resembled the sound of a sweet, divine flute. The seeker asked himself, "Is this the flute of the Supreme?"

The purity in the air was one of the most beautiful. The feeling of flying was no better than that of walking. Being a winged being in that place, the seeker understood the real meaning of compassion for those who still live below in illusion. For a moment, he identified with the eagle that flies higher. Finally, he found his home, for none of the places he had passed through had ever been as familiar as this one. In his homeland, he saw himself as a stranger, and now, being in the clouds, he thought, "I have wandered from continent to continent to finally find the promised land within myself. Now what to do? O Eternal Creator, what a burning desire to want to remain here forever!"

The seeker remembered all that the master had told him about the identity of the Being. He said, "After sailing the oceans for so long, men have forgotten that without water, the sea would be nothing but an immense void. Ignorance has invaded the human intellect, and today men feel proud of having a soul." The master also said, "How can mortality contain immortality?" Until then, the seeker had not understood the master's words, but at that moment, everything became clear, for he realized that a body without a soul was like an ocean devoid of water. As he could fly so high and still feel his feet on the ground, he consecrated himself as a Soul. Then he thought, "I do not have a soul. I am a Soul. I possess bodies, and I exist because the Supreme Being loves me." He intuited that in that place, there was no human consciousness but Soul consciousness. As a Soul, he felt united with all creation. Within himself, there was no conflict, for he could contemplate the Supreme Truth without needing to think about it. It was nothing more than action consolidated in inaction. It became clear to him that the concept of genuine being is beyond the realm of the mind. Thus he understood that the Soul has no gender, creed, religion, culture, or tradition, and despite its youthful spirit, It remains eternal.

In conclusion, the seeker perceived that the Love that bound him to the world was immeasurable. That experience conveyed to him that the Soul, without any distinction, loves everyone just as it loves its True Father.

If you must choose between extravagant actions and humble words to honor charity, choose humility, for, through it, the Soul manifests Itself.

What did you see?

The next day Eduardo woke up, serene, in his host's house. This time he became a new man. The understanding of his inner journey showed on his face a clarity he had never experienced before. The doubts in his mind were gone, and along with them, the fear was gone too. "What is left of a man who no longer fears?" the seeker asked himself.

A voice that had been silent for a long time answered him, "He who does not fear only loves. If you look with eyes that do not judge, you will see Love in all things, everywhere in the universe, and far beyond. Whether in dream or reality, Love makes beings vibrate. It is the breath of all life forms. The man who cannot see Love in abundance and scarcity is certainly blind and will not see himself. He will not live fully and will remain a slave to the mental passions. Then, if he genuinely loves, with nothing to judge, nothing to desire, nothing to regret, nothing to hope for, and nothing to demand, he will establish himself above the lack and the abundance of all things. Life after life, man lives asleep, trying to escape from himself. However, Love has never given up on him. Love is like the great sun that gives its light to all without discrimination or preference."

Very clearly, Eduardo recognized in this voice the singular voice that first made him leave home. Through this sound, he perceived the healing for his anxious spirit and the expression of the Golden Heart. It became evident to the new man that the purpose of Life is to LOVE.

Then he got out of bed and sat down on the floor, imitating the posture of a monk already preparing to contemplate. But first, he felt the need to remember the moments when he had not lived fully. The master had already said, "Live and reflect, for in reflection lies the true meaning of life."

Eduardo then began to remember — of the moments he stopped smiling at strangers on the street; of all the masks he had to wear to be accepted; of all the paths he stopped following because someone said it was not the right one; of all the nights he exchanged rest for torment and lamentation; of the times he judged strangers; of the moments he kept silent in the face of injustice; of the lies told for the sake of fame and power; of the promises made in vain; of the moments in which he preferred the hypocrisy of a thousand women to the sincere love of only one; of the moments in which he blamed his parents for his own mistakes; of the moments in which he considered a simple criticism as a great offense; of the times in which he surrendered to fear; of the days in which he stopped observing the grandiosity of nature by constantly complaining about the cold or the heat; of the past lives in which he ignored the divine laws.

After contemplating, Eduardo seemed aware of what he was meant to do. He got up and began to pack. At that moment, his host, Mr. João, entered the house.

"Good morning, Eduardo. Are you abandoning us already?"

"Yes, Mr. João. Fortunately, or unfortunately, I will have to continue the journey. I am eternally grateful for the fact that you sheltered me in your house."

"Where are you going now?" ask Mr. João.

"I am going where I was born. The Capital of the Central Lands is in crisis. Human corruption destroyed it. I believe I can help my people to regain a taste for life. Since everything has been demolished, we need to rebuild everything. We need to redefine our concepts and values. My brothers no longer know who they are. I miss the wisdom that hovered over my homeland. However, I no longer live from the past. So I want to help in this process of reconstruction, both physically and spiritually."

"You know, Eduardo, I always thought that this was your natural home. In other lands, men are cruel to each other. In your place, I would not risk happiness here. I know that our satisfaction in Kunda is limited, but it is the best I know in the world."

"Do you believe in the goodness of the men here?"

"Yes, I do," answered Mr. João.

"As far as I know, the men in this village are not only part of the Central Lands, but also the world. I ask, then, how come you do not believe in the world while you believe in some men who are part of it?" With a wry whisper, Mr. João replied, "I do not know what to say."

"O my friend, I apologize for my lack of delicateness. Before I leave, I have a few questions. I believe that the answers will help us, in a way, to better face life," said Eduardo.

"The years have convinced me not to chase time, so I am not in a hurry. Ask me your questions."

"Mr. João, where is our true home? Where is genuine peace found? Is it in the realm of Earth or Heaven?"

"It seems that only the Creator knows the Truth of the world. But as long as we live in the kingdom of men, our home is our happiness. But for me, there is no happiness anywhere else but here. If I had a way to escape from men, I would have done it long ago."

"You say you want to run away from men, but aren't you also a man? Would you run away from yourself?" asked Eduardo.

"I do not know what to think anymore. I live in the antagonism of my being. Sometimes I do not recognize myself. One day I am happy, and the next, unhappy, no matter if I am at home or someone else's place. I have been wondering where the true peace that I have so unsuccessfully sought is. Every night when I lie in bed, I wait for the wind to take me to where I belong because deep in my heart, I do not doubt that the Earth is only my refuge. Within human consciousness, I am running away from myself. As for my true home, that place where perhaps I will find complete happiness, all I can say is that my eyes still cannot see the hidden Truth. When I praise the Creator, I wait for the candles to be burned out, for the Truth to be revealed to me. However, with each expectation of mine, comes a new frustration, and so life goes on."

"Mr. João, I believe with all humility that happiness is neither here nor there. The path to happiness is within us. Know and feel yourself, and you will know your history. Then you will realize that you have always been in the heart of the One who has never stopped loving you. He is our True Father."

"Eduardo, your words sound like the melody of the heart. Everything in me, thank you for your kindness. We here on the mountain are used to Haroldo's comings and goings. But I do not know if my family and I can get used to your absence."

With a puzzled look on his face, Eduardo asked, "Is Samah's friend not a native of Kunda?"

"No, my friend. It is unknown where Haroldo comes from, but from time to time, he appears. We nicknamed him 'Samah's friend' because he takes over the mountain every time he comes. And every time he shows up, a stranger mysteriously appears. As for my family, our tradition has always been to welcome strangers into our home. Of all the travelers who have stepped foot in this abode, you are the first to become my friend. Almost non-existent were our conversations, but the admiration I hold for you is great."

Immediately, Eduardo remembered that time when the master said, "Our meeting is the answer to an equation, (...)"

The seeker, more resolute than ever, looked tenderly at his host and said, "Mr. João, know that everything is in its proper place. In this world, nothing happens by chance. For everything, there is a cause. Sometimes, what seems unfair to us is, in fact, the expression of Justice. What is effect today, becomes cause tomorrow. This moves the wheel of lives that never stops turning. Life after life, death comes to close men's eyes, so one day they can contemplate the Supreme Truth. When man stops separating night from day, he will begin to see things in their totality. He will understand the No-thing and the Every-thing by Unity. And by Unity he will love all as he loves himself."

"Your wisdom is worthy of a king."

"Mr. João, every man who chooses to love rather than to reign, will become genuine by nature, and will regally guide his heart to the Glory of glories. Here, our story ends, so a new journey can happen. I am already leaving. Pass my love on to your family and know that I will always be with you."

"As for Cindi? What do you want me to tell her? Of my daughters, she is the most attached to you. I feel sorry for her already."

"Tell her that we will meet again, as we have done so many times before. Tell her also that we are souls, and this world is too small for us."

"Eduardo, before you go, tell me, what did you see?"

The seeker remained silent for a few minutes.

"It is fine if you do not want to answer."

Eduardo finally said, "What I saw escapes the eyes, what I heard escapes the ears, and what I understood escapes the thoughts. Well, Mr. João, the truth is that I saw something, but I could not differentiate the night from the day. Forgive me, but there are no words to describe the feeling of becoming myself."

With a long hug, the two men said goodbye. Eduardo left. Then, Mr. João sat down in the middle of the room and began to reflect on their conversation. On the other hand, as soon as Eduardo hit the road, he began to hear an inward melody, like that of his heavenly trip. In a spirit of contentment, the man looked at the sky as he walked. At some point, he began to hum a chant that he had learned in the Second Country of the Eastern Lands:

The universe is singing
the melody of the Soul
I am walking the path
that leads to my door
I must open it
with inner love
The prodigal son
won't fall again

The eyes of the heart

A few hours after setting out on his way home, the seeker saw a man who seemed unbalanced. He was talking to himself, saying things that seemed to have no connection between them. Eduardo quickly remembered his conversation with old Bokô in the Southlands. Looking thin, the stranger approached him and asked, "Who are you?" The seeker, after a moment, answered, "I am everybody, I am nobody."

The stranger looked at Eduardo and said, "I am crazy, and I know my dementia. I am hideous, and I know my ugliness. That is why everyone looks down on me when they cross my path, but you...," with a short breath, the stranger continued, "You looked at me smiling, a luminous smile that reminded me of the brightness of a thousand suns. You did not judge me. You just saw me with the eyes of your heart. Do you know who you are to me?"

Staggered, Eduardo asked, "Who am I to you?" The man replied, "You are my way, the way of the heart. The path that the prodigal son walks toward the Absolute Father. For the heart that loves, knows the Genuine Truth. May the blessings accompany you until you reach your heart. There is your eternal dwelling."

With these words, the stranger went on his way. Eduardo did the same. He looked back from time to time, and there was the mountain Samah, which looked back at him. This is how it went until he was entirely away from Kunda. Again, he looked back, and there was no more Samah. He then knew that he must concentrate on the path, for what really matters is the journey itself — the Now.

The end

Follow my publications on Instagram:

@herlicpoemas

9 786500 647051